The Best Man

The Best Man

Selections from the First Three Years
of MAN! Magazine

edited by Sharon Adams

Mandala Publications
Austin, Texas

Introduction and selection copyright © 1992 by Mandala Publications
Printed in the United States of America

Book Design by Forrest Taftyn
Cover Design by Bill Jeffers and Sharon Adams
ISBN# 0-9633927-3-5

For Dad

Contents

Chapter IV: Family Man

Chapter V: Political Man

Chapter VI: Spiritual Man

Chapter VII: Cultural/Social Man

Chapter VIII: Recovering Man

Chapter IX: Men In Our Lives

Foreword

Being the editor and publisher of a magazine is not all it is cracked up to be. And it is much, much more. When my wife, Sharon, my friend John Lee and I decided to create a journal for men, we had already turned the four-page newsletter of the Austin Men's Center into a 24-page newsletter. Although all three of us had writing experience, no one had any real, practical knowledge or experience in how to run the business of a magazine. We were scared, but our dream of producing a beautiful, thoughtful, helpful, and inspiring magazine about men was stronger.

And right there — for me, at least — is the meaning and importance of this magazine called **MAN!** and the importance of the men's movement and the recovery movement, from which we draw our inspiration. Dare to dream, these movements tell us. Dare to act upon that dream. And when the dream does not come true in six weeks, dare to live the nightmares that accompany the dream. Don't be stupid, we learn. Always examine the truth about what you are committed to; always examine your reasons for pursuing the dream; always listen to your detractors; but always listen to your heart, too.

In understanding and pursuing this dream, **MAN!** has been blessed both by the patience and provocations of its readers. Although our readers have been overwhelmingly supportive, we have occasionally angered them. The most rageful of these readers are provoked by the fact that we have women on our staff. The fact is that many men have been abused by women and feel vulnerable by their mere presence. These men need to be recognized and supported. And the women who abuse people — whatever gender — must stop. However, sometimes these angry men wish to generalize and say something like "All women are abusers," a statement we cannot support.

Ironically, we owe our greatest thanks to these two or three men who persistently harangued us for about six months. They forced us to develop a stronger, clearer editorial position. We had known that **MAN!** would not be always politically correct, and that **MAN!** would avoid partisan politics, because we viewed the us/them system a symptom of our overall malaise. Still until then we had maintained a *Field of Dreams* philosophy — "build it and they will come." Well, they came, and these men forced us to examine what statements the magazine would support, which it would tolerate, and which it would denounce.

The following essay, originally titled "What is MAN?," is my response to those men who wrote to us complaining about the women on our staff. Published in the Summer 1991 issue, we include it here because it is the most complete statement about the guiding philosophy behind MAN! and the work that we print.

What is MAN!?

For the first time in history, we can have a human story, not a tribal story.
— Robert Moore

I suppose every so often it is good for the soul to search it — to take the scalpel to one's psyche; to probe into the cartilage of one's spirit wings; to grasp and squeeze, bloody-handed, one's soul organs.

Every so often someone writes a letter to us or calls with a question or concern that forces the knife into my hands and commands incision. Why MAN!? What are the values that I impart into MAN!? To what does MAN! say the Everlasting Yea and to what the Everlasting Nay? These are big questions, and every time I consider them I am thrown back into the ashes. As Robert Bly has pointed out in *Iron John*, these questions send one back into the kitchen, back into one's grief, into the rot and scraps of one's life.

So what do I find there in the trail of trash I leave behind me? I find a father who talked about "good niggers" and "bad niggers." I find a mother who whipped me with her father's razor strop and who, more than my father, accepted me only when I behaved like a "good young soldier." I find a high school girlfriend who broke up with me two times so she could date a football player. I find two women I treated cruelly 15 years ago, but who still remain my friends. I find a sister who, during one of the lowest periods of my life, gave me a silly gift that renewed my faith in myself. I find a college professor who gave me an F to teach me a lesson about punctuality. I find a gay professor who, because I liked Shakespeare, made me a gift of his father's 40-volume set, published in the 19th century. I find another gay man from Big Sandy, Texas, who cooked the best spoon bread I've ever eaten, who quoted reams of Tennessee Williams to me and called me the "Plumed Hat Cavalier," and who never once made a sexual overture to me.

I find two dead parents, an abortion I walked away from, my hopes of being a poet deferred for decades, a marriage that rocks back and forth. I find students I have been unavailable to, a son I have occasionally whipped, a black schoolmate I insulted 25 years ago, and a score of women who should hate me. I find. . . You get the point.

So when I receive letters that "get under my skin," I really get irritated. There are a lot of tender places for them to rub against. But the letters that sting me the most are those that criticize our practice of including women and gays in the circle of **MAN!**, including them as friends and supporters, including them as people who can teach us about manhood, including them as victims and as perpetrators.

To all you men — and I don't think there are very many — who want **MAN!** to blame all men's troubles on feminism, I tell you once and for all, NO! To all you men — and again there are a few of you — who want **MAN!** to denounce gays as some sort of sick aberration of the male gender, I tell you NO!

My experience as a man tells me there is enough blame and hatred to devastate us all. My experience of feminism has taught me much. One of the most important lessons is how much it hurts to be blamed as a man for all the troubles that women have. I do not wish to return the favor.

My experience of healing old wounds, however, tells me that hate and blame are wonderful tonics when they are named and attached to deserving individuals. I hate my mother for whipping me. To the extent I allow myself to admit that hate, the less likely I am to hit my son and the less likely I am to accept false blame from my wife.

My experience of joy tells me that it is delivered in unlikely hands. If I were to hate all gays, I would have one less way to understand myself, as a "Plumed Hat Cavalier." Nor would I own the 40 volumes of Shakespeare that sit across from me now as I write. If I were to fear the touch of another man, I would. . . I can't imagine the sorrow in that.

So if **MAN!** says NO to generalized hate and blame, what do we say YES to? Like Walt Whitman, Henry Thoreau, D.H. Lawrence, Henry Miller, Dionysus, Zorba the Greek, **MAN!** says YES to the experience and to the feelings. We say YES to joy and anger, to grief and ecstasy. We say YES to the man who feels hatred because his ex-wife denies him contact with his children. We say YES to the man who wants to discard his coat and tie to drum and dance. We say YES to the soft, naive man who strives to become a warrior for a noble cause. We say YES to the Vietnam veterans and the humiliation they felt when the protesters spat on them. We say YES to those who lost sons, brothers and fathers in the war. We say YES to the man who grieves the loss of a father who could not love him. We say YES to the man who celebrates the renewed relationship with his lost father.

My experience in saying YES to each experience and feeling, to the ugly and the good, is that the ugly passes away and the good remains. When the anger and the grief, the humiliation and the shame, are fully acknowledged and felt, they fall away and give rise to joy.

It seems to me that the world cries desperately for unity. As Robert Moore says, the time of tribalism is over. The world's healing and salvation lie not in a narrow, tribal, or single-sex mythology, but in a larger mythology that awaits creation. Alone, men cannot heal the world nor even themselves. There are things that we need to do in the company of men, but our work always serves a greater healing. Yes, I say YES to the anger I sometimes feel toward my mother and father. I say YES to the thousand sorrows of my life as a man. I say YES to the painful probing and poking of my soul that leads to my healing. And I say YES to the ecstasy of the great reunion, of which, because of the courage of our readers and writers, I sometimes glimpse in the pages of **MAN!** Peace.

As this book is published, **MAN!** will be completing its fourth year. Like the men's movement — like men in general — **MAN!** is a work in progress, and *The Best Man* represents a stage in that progress. In an early issue, Robert Bly warned us against being naive. Later, Randolf Severson praised for us the courage of men. Even later, James Sniechowski told us that men were daring to create a new definition for masculinity. These are the positive voices, among many others, that John, Sharon, and I listen to as we continue to follow our dream.

Nowadays, we dream about a world where each man can become what he desires to be, about a world where each woman can become what she desires to be, about a world where each child feels fully loved and totally safe, where each parent feels completely supported, and where each citizen feels a commitment to and a commitment from his or her community and its institutions. Dare we dream of anything less?

With this celebratory volume, I want to say thank you to all the people who have helped make the **MAN!** dream survive. To Bill Jeffers, Forrest Taftyn, Jodi Roberts, Jean Barnett, Allen Maurer, Tom Sandlin,

Kitty Kirkpatrick, David Kramer, and Jeff King, we owe great thanks. I also need to bow to Frank and Jan King, Dan Jones, Bill Stott, Claud Payne, Tim Grear, and John Hunger. I particularly thank my partners. John Lee is a spiritual partner, the older brother I never had. Sharon is a true life-partner, my missing half that I am reunited on earth with. Her knowledge is broad; her eye is sharp; her insights are deep; her love is strong. Without her, **MAN!** would have folded long ago. She works when everyone else is tired, and she gives me courage to find the light when the dream turns dark. I am not insulting her or men when I say she is the woman behind *The Best MAN*.

LYMAN GRANT

Preface

The Best Man is a collection of essays, interviews, articles and poems selected from the first three years of **MAN!** Magazine. For readers of **MAN!**, it will be no surprise that while all the pieces are about men, there is a great diversity of viewpoint and focus. There are, after all, as many different stories as there are men, each with its own vision of the man and his sense of masculinity. In **MAN!** we search for the many new models for modern man being lived on our streets and in our homes. Some of our articles look at the psychology of men, some at family relationships, some are concerned with modern cultural patterns and others examine myths and stories from the past. There seems to be no typical man in our world today, and we reflect this diversity in the magazine.

As a woman, the experience of working on **MAN!** has greatly expanded my perceptions about men. The voices of our readers, men and women, speak every day in letters, phone calls, and contributions. They are not the voices I hear on television or in the news. They are usually not the men and women of the fashion press, the powerful presences of government and business, nor the experts of academic disciplines. But they send clear, thoughtful, heartfelt messages, sometimes angry, sometimes painful, sometimes hopeful about men and women and the world. It is to these readers, this audience, we direct our magazine and this book.

Few would argue that women's roles have not undergone monumental changes during the past 40 years. Less evident is the place for men in this new world. While many feel that the old forms of masculinity, those models we knew from the '40s and '50s, are obsolete, no new positive images for men have come clearly into view. In their place we see a hazy mix of oppressive, uncaring brutes or helpless, ineffectual bumblers. It is not only the media who portray these pictures, but everyday interaction with men and women provides recurring disparaging references to some generic "he" who is inherently responsible for the mess we're all in. The reality, of course, is far more complex.

A mosaic of the several models of the modern male emerges from the pages of **MAN!** Friends, brothers, lovers and friends are remembered in the "Men in Our Lives" readers' forum. Cultural roles, political structures and employment hierarchies are examined with a particular look at the parts men play and how they are affected by them. We catch a glimpse of personal relationships and their intricate patterns of power, intimacy, pain and joy. There is some humor — we would like to see more — that offers that saving dose of laughter that male companionship can provide.

As with most such selective offerings, we found it difficult to exclude some of the fine pieces that have appeared in the past three years. Several of our favorites by well-known writers were omitted because they can be found in other publications. In particular, Wendell Berry's piece, "Men and Women: Living and Working Together" (excerpted from *What Are People For?* published by North Point Press); Michael Ventura's "White Boys Dancing" (from *Shadow Dancing in the USA*, published by Jeremy Tarcher) and Sam Keen's "Vocation and Virility" (from *Fire in the Belly*, published by Bantam Books), helped us define the magazine's vision and direction. I should add that reader responses to these and other essays did as much to clarify our thinking as did the original writing.

Several of our favorite reader contributions to "Men in Our Lives" are not in this book because we were unable to contact the authors for reprint permission. Some excellent writing was not included when we felt it repeated a theme already in the collection.

In producing a book, just as in producing a magazine, you find that you have a large family to thank. I want to especially thank the staff at **MAN!** Many of them also contributed to the production of this book. I especially want to thank Forrest Taftyn, who typeset and designed this book, and Bill Jeffers, who designed the cover.

Special thanks goes to my husband, Lyman Grant, and my friend, John Lee, whom I have joined in this creative venture. And I would like to acknowledge my seven-year-old son, Will, who has taught me more about the energy, power and vulnerability of a young boy than a lifetime of reading and thinking could provide.

SHARON ADAMS

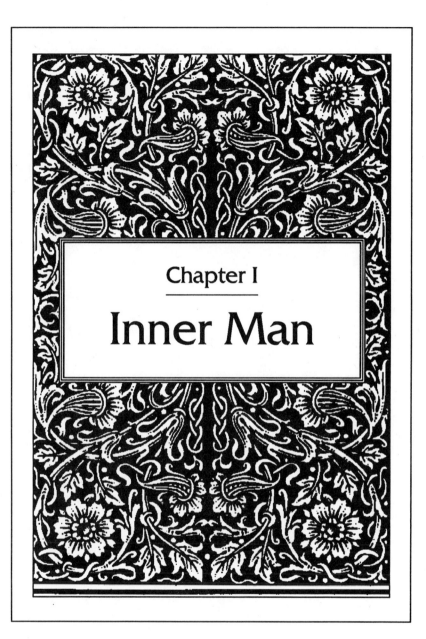

Chapter I

Inner Man

Male Naiveté
and the
Loss of the Kingdom

by Robert Bly

Naiveté

I'll tell you a fairy story called "The Devil's Sooty Brother" from the Grimm collection. The word "devil" was doubtless added in Christian times to a tale probably hundreds of years older, so one needn't put too much attention on that word. Another title would be "The Dark Man's Sooty Brother." The character referred to, whom you'll soon meet, is very likely an ancient god, probably an old earth god, identified as such by his animal foot.

I remember Joseph Campbell saying, "The important thing is not merely living, but finding out which myth you are living, so you can live it more intelligently and completely. Later you might try to find out which myth is living you." The myth I'll tell is unlikely to be your myth, but it may be.

Once upon a time there was a soldier who had just been discharged. While walking in the woods, in that curious state mingling freedom and loneliness that we feel after having been discharged from a job, he met a man with an odd-shaped foot. "Why are you sad?" "I don't know what to do next." "You could work for me." "What is the work?" "You would live underground at my place and spend seven years tending my three pots, and keeping them boiling. You will not look into the pots. During that time you cannot cut your fingernails or your toenails nor your hair, nor wipe the tears from your eyes. The shavings you will sweep behind the door. Can you do it?" "I think so." "You're hired. Good. I'll come back once in a while to see how you're doing."

So the man began work. He chopped wood, swept the shavings behind the door, put the wood chunks under the three pots, which were

3

huge and black with covers, and so kept the fires going. After three or four months, he said to himself, "I think I'll peek into the first pot." He did, and to his surprise he saw his sergeant sitting there. "Oh ho!" he said. "You had me in your power, but now I have you in my power." And he added more wood to that fire. He worked a few more months and then felt the desire to peek into the second pot. He did, and saw his lieutenant sitting there. "Ah ha!" he said. "You once had me in your power; but now I have you in my power." And he added a lot more wood to that fire. Six months later or so he couldn't resist his longing to peek into the third pot. He lifted the cover and who did he see but his old general—General Westmoreland! — sitting in that pot. "Well, well," he said. "Once you had me in your power; but now I have you in my power." He chopped extra wood and added good, dry oak under that pot.

When the Dark Man returned to see how the work was going, he remarked, "By the way, you looked into the pots, and if you hadn't added more wood, I really would have punished you for that."

Time seemed to pass faster now, what with the extra chopping each day, and week by week the time went by, and the seven years were up.

The Dark Man returned and said, "You've done your work well." He swept up some of the shavings behind the door, put them in a gunny sack, gave the sack to the man, and said, "Here are your wages." The man was disappointed, but what can you do? Always remember to arrange your wages beforehand. The Dark One said: "When anyone asks you who you are from now on, you are to say, 'I am the Dark Man's Sooty Brother and my King as well.'" It didn't really make sense, but he memorized the sentence and prepared to go back to the world.

He left the workplace and the strangest thing was this: as he made his way up to our world, the shavings in his bag all turned to gold. That pleased him, of course. Eventually, he came to an Inn, and asked for a room. The Innkeeper said, "Who are you?" He said, "I am the Dark Man's Sooty Brother and my King as well." He hadn't shaved for seven years, nor wiped the tears from his eyes — you remember that — so the Innkeeper did not find him to be an appetizing guest, and said, "I'm sorry, but I have no rooms left for tonight." Then this worker made his first mistake — he opened the sack and showed the Innkeeper the gold. The Innkeeper now said, "Well, as I think of it, I remember that my brother, who has been in #10, is going away this weekend, and you can have his room tonight." So it was. In the middle of the night the Innkeeper crept into the room and stole the gold. That's the way it goes. Our friend felt bad about it, but he said to himself: "It was through no fault of mine," and he decided to go back underground. He did go down and asked the Dark Man for more wages. "That's not a big problem," said the Dark Man, sweeping up another shovelful of shavings. He put them into a bag, and that was that. Then our friend said something else to the Dark Man: "Sit down and trim my fingernails and my toenails. After that, shave me and cut my hair." These people have to be asked, you know. The Dark Man did all that.

This chopper of wood now went to the upper world once more, and this time he knew more about innkeepers. He made his living travelling around the country and performing music on an instrument that he had learned to play while underground. Eventually, the King of that country heard about his music, invited him to the castle, and you know how such things go — the King's daughter found the musician attractive. It wasn't long before the King realized the way the clouds were moving, and he said, "If you choose to marry my daughter, you will get half my kingdom, and after I die, the whole of it." That seemed to be a good prospect, so the musician did just that; and after the King died, he inherited the entire kingdom. What luck he had! But I must tell you that my luck hasn't changed at all, and I still walk from place to place with holes in my socks. I don't know if you are more like me or him, but the story is over.

As we think back over this story, we notice a number of themes that deserve some comment. The story embodies the old mythological theme of male descent, and suggests some form of initiation for young men, guided by the old earth god. Most of us know the Sumerian story of Innana's descent, which is a model for many feminine descents into the underworld, but less attention has been paid to the masculine descent. Hercules participates in that descent, also Gilgamesh and Joseph, who went down to "Egypt." In our story, it is interesting that the man who descends retains as well some qualities of the Wild Man — long hair, uncut nails, and unconcealed grief.

The man who descends has to keep kettles boiling — that is his labor. It turns out that the "shavings" are important. The instructions are precise: sweep the shavings behind the door. If we try that, we find that when we open the door to let our friends or enemies in, the shavings will not be visible, for the opened door will hide them; but when the visitors leave and we close the door once more, all these shavings will be visible to our own eyes once more. So the story recommends a beautiful little dance of hiding and revealing.

Certain insights come to us when we are in depression; a therapist may guide us to other insights, or the labor that we go through making a work of art may produce other shavings. The insights don't seem particularly precious when they arrive. They are part of the work, that is the chopping—but when we come back up into the "day world," the story says each shaving turns to gold. That seems right. What are we chopping? Perhaps chunks of wood from the hill or our particular childhood, blocks of our shame.

The chunks of wood — split from our childhood — have a use: they keep the pots boiling. It turns out that our old sergeants, lieutenants and generals sit in these pots that we have been asked by the old earth god to keep boiling. I think it's important to say that the sooty brother is not boiling people — after all, there are no people in a fairy story. All the characters are acting inside a single psyche — our own. What he sees in the pot is then not a person, but an image — we could say an image of authority. Those who haven't served in the army may find instead a high school principal sitting there, an aunt, a coach, a thesis advisor, the critic who humiliated you when you showed him your first poems. Usually these figures lie over us, on top of us, pressing down rather than sitting in a pot; and we are passive beneath them, inert, resigned, stuck.

The story says that being passive beneath such authority figures is not the thing — one has to be active toward them, boil them. That requires an underground place, a pot, the hard work of chopping, heat, ashes, soot.

We know that if one boils milk for hours, as the cowherds do in Norway, one will get cheese, highly concentrated. Apparently these images transform when they are boiled as well. The old, still-controlling power of the authority figures gets boiled away. "Once I was in your power; now you are in my power." Boiling pulls them from the outer world into our own psychic skin, where they respond to our impulses and are in our power. Such boiling amounts to shrewdness and activity.

There is still the matter of naiveté. Why is it that the young male is still naive after he has gone through this complicated process of boiling? Why is that? The old earth god has warned him not to be inflated. When he goes out into the world and is asked who he is, he is not to say: "I have spent three years at the Jung Institute in Zurich and I am a licensed

Jungian psychotherapist," or "I am a Quaker since birth and now an Overseer in my Friends Meeting," or "I am a student of Tibetan Buddhism" — such answers would be dangerous. He is to say: "I am the Dark Man's Sooty Brother and my King as well." So his relative isn't the Dark Man's shiny brother, but the Dark Man's Sooty Brother, and he is "my King as well." This phrase, as oblique in German as it is in English, suggests that the process of boiling has freed him from some reliance on outer authority or outer kingship, so that he is his own king. So far, so good. Despite the change in his attitude toward outward authority, he is still naive. He shows the gold shavings to the Innkeeper.

This is a sad mistake — we will return to it. This is the moment I want you to notice. Many other scenes of the story deserve more comment than we will give them. On his second visit, the youth orders the Dark Man to cut his hair and cut his fingernails; this implies his new confidence in relation to the Underworld. That moment is delicious. It turns out that while in the Underworld he has learned to play a musical instrument; and music leads to a connection with the "King's Daughter," who is as mysterious in this story as in most others. That in turn leads to his receiving his own "kingdom." I will leave you to speculate on these lucky connections.

I've told this story because the scene in which the gold shavings are lost conveys the mood of male naiveté.

We could say that naiveté is a state of feeling which avoids the dark side of one's own motives or the motives of others. Naiveté discounts anger, fear or greed, and assumes more goodness in the world than there is. The naive person often refuses confrontation or combat, and if thrown into it by circumstances, often fails to notice the moment of defeat. Wearing white armor, he goes off with the defeated army, waving as if he were a victor.

Naiveté seems to be characteristic of men in the New Age, but it is not peculiar to them. Naiveté is a product of a failure in initiation. It seems to me more common in men than in women. Women seem to have some edge of shrewdness in personal relationships. A daughter sometimes has to become shrewd to get from her mother what the mother gives freely to the son. Men seem to have some edge in shrewdness in their dealings with the outer world.

In naiveté, there is a porous container or none at all. The naive man in a relationship does not keep a good container around himself; he can't imagine why one should need a container or a shield. Something has dissolved his shield; if he has one, he throws it down in each encounter. When he is fighting with a woman or a man, and insults are flying, he may open his body to the attacks, throw his arms wide, invite in the damaging opinions, allow his chest to become a target for lances, so that he ends up with six or seven lances sticking out of his body as he promises to do better, be more thoughtful, less sexist, etc.

We can imagine manners and courtesy as a verbal container. When a visitor comes to the door in Japan, the host may say, "For a humble person such as myself it is an honor for me and all my ancestors to greet the celestial person that you are." He doesn't believe a word of it, but the sentence serves well as a container, reminding both parties of the space around each of them that is appropriate. Manners prevent inappropriate mergings and make invasion of the psyche less likely. We recognize the naive person as characteristically American; and Americans, as Europeans often remark, have few or no manners. This lack of manners is highly dangerous; the naive man talks too much. Goethe in his poem "Holy Longing," says:

Tell a wise person, or else keep silent,
because the mass man will mock it right away.

The naive person doesn't fear the mass man; and may idealize him. At a party, he tells strangers his most intimate experiences.

You'll notice that the Dark Man's apprentice opens the bag and shows its contents to what we could call the False Innkeeper. Some being in the universe called the False Innkeeper is forced to steal the gold. He has no choice. He can take the form of a student who asks you flattering questions, a person at the office who draws out your indiscreet opinions of others, a talk-show host. "Let's tell everything." The talker will wake up in the morning with the bag empty. "During this weekend," says the encounter leader, "I want you to get everything out." The group mind says: "Come on, tell us!"

The Romans had a name for the particular soul-being of each person, the genetic identity unaffected by environment. The name used was "genius" in a man, "juno" in a woman. We could say then that the naive man, to stay with him for a moment, fails to respect his own genius. He tells secret dreams to strangers, imagines he can achieve art without discipline, regards all boundaries as evil, ignores ancestors, wants comfort and merging, believes cunning is wrong, and as a scholar or artist doesn't develop the persistence necessary to create works solid enough to justify his own genius.

The naive man often values "sincerity" above all else, and prizes simple major chords above complicated minor chords. "I don't understand why she left me. I did betray her with other women, but I was sincere when I told her about it." He thinks his sincerity should protect him from a long look at the shadow side. He enters a tunnel without noticing the shadow side of tunnels, or the tendency of a tunnel to become narrower and darker. "Let's hope for the best." The way American politicians entered the tunnel called the Vietnam War was highly naive; the Russian politicians were equally naive in entering Afghanistan.

When naiveté spreads to parenting, we have the characteristic American permissive parent. Naiveté throws away self-authority. In child-raising it amounts to becoming a servant of the child. The father becomes a "pal." He does not state his expectations, sets no limits, agrees that duties are negotiable, gives too many objects to the child. It's clear that such naive parenting is a disease in the United States.

Naive man loves the word "wholeness," even though no one is whole. All this talk of wholeness, then holistic world views, wholeness and healing, Whole Earth Catalog, holistic health, "every fragment contains the whole," "holistic relationship," etc. encourages naiveté, and inflames the False Innkeeper to outrageous acts of theft. Naiveté works hand-in-hand with the False Innkeeper to cloud the issue, disappoint the psychic worker, mess up contracts. The naive man trusts the charismatic leader, such as Ronald Reagan, who immediately steals the gold. He trusts his boss and the boss overworks him. His children turn him into a slave, his wife forces him to do what she wants him to do, and so on.

Passivity

A close relative of naiveté in contemporary men is passivity. Passivity can be thought of as a second product of the absence or interruption of the initiation process. The male consciousness becomes stagnated at an early level, and the man's emotional body does not become activated. The boy's constant play activates the physical body, but it has always been the job of initiation to activate the emotional body.

The old men, who still today initiate boys in Australian aborigine tribes and in New Guinea and African tribes, take the boys away from the mothers between the ages of eight and 12 and begin a complicated sequence of adventures, trials, and dances. The old men recite poems, act out myths, sing, say outrageous things, and may themselves dance for hours or dance all night. The boys experience close up what the emotional body of a man is like when it is activated. The boys themselves are taught to dance in some tribes for 24 hours straight. But the old men in this country are not activating the emotional bodies of the young men. The young men in the last decades have tried to do it for themselves through rock music or gang activity, but it does not succeed. Only old men can do it, and the old men are in business.

Many men, as I've heard participants at men's conferences say repeatedly, have no model of the activated male. Some men describe scenes in childhood in which the mother flew into a rage, directed at the father or at the boy, and their fathers said nothing, sank into silence and guilt, or disappeared from the room, defending neither themselves nor their sons. Such a boy, when he grows up, will probably not be able to hold his boundaries. He may alternate between abusive behavior that is violent, and an impotent gentleness that isn't really gentle. Robert Moore has remarked that two marks of the uninitiated man are wife beating on one side and too much softness on the other.

There are exceptions, of course, but a woman's emotional body and her physical body seem to be better interwoven, and that happens at an early age. I saw a group of seventh-grade children the other day singing in the nave of a church. The girls' bodies swayed naturally to the rhythm, and the boys without exception stood stiffly as they sang. A woman in menstruation will observe emotional changes swiftly following from physical changes. The emotional bodies of women often seem to glow through the physical bodies. An emotional perception may appear as a body response, a pain in one arm, a heat in the chest.

A woman who notices that a man's emotional body is not activated will sometimes offer to activate it for him, by helping him to express his feelings, or teaching him to be more sensual. It may be that sex deepens the integration of physical and emotional bodies in a woman, but the same thing doesn't seem to work for a man. In general, I would say that the emotional body of a man cannot be activated by a woman. That's precisely why the old men undertake that activity. In some cultures, the older men give years and years of their lives to doing just that.

If a man's emotional body has not been activated, then he will let girlfriends or wives take the lead in many areas of relationship. He may not be able to talk about his feelings; he may not recognize certain emotions, such as anger, when he has them; he may not know how to fight fruitfully with a woman.

When the woman expresses anger, a man may give in right away, or in a contrary way refuse to engage at all, saying, "Oh, you're just being. . ." A man with weak boundaries may take into himself the jibes and criticisms thrown, and retire with wounded feelings that last for days. The passive man is so unfamiliar with feelings that when a woman throws anger at him he receives those feelings as if they came from God or his mother, and he loses the springiness essential to good fighting. He doesn't believe in fighting at home. Jung remarked, "American marriages are the saddest in all the world, because the man does all his fighting at the office."

The passive man, then, or the man whose emotional body is not activated, will live through years of a relationship secretly resentful, dimly enraged, passively hostile.

More and more men in the United States now allow a corporation to choose where they will live, what their politics are, even how they will dress. Approximately 90 percent of American men at the turn of the century were independent farmers who made most major decisions themselves. Recent research reports that 48 percent of American men are now employed either by one of the top 10 giant corporations or by the United States government. We have to expect that passivity will deepen. Writers in Eastern Europe, where a characteristic state bureaucracy has been in force for several generations, have described in Kafka-like terms the passive hostility, mingling resentment, malice and shame, that result from bureaucratic control. Kafka writes in *Metamorphosis*, "As Gregor Samsa awoke one morning from uneasy dreams, he found himself transformed in his bed into a gigantic insect." Ollie North's story makes clear that furious and independent activity in one area does not rule out a sheeplike and passive attitude toward higher authority in another.

Fundamentalist religions require a dependent mind. Disciples in Oregon allow the guru to do all the Rolls Royce owning; devoted traditionalists allow Jimmy Swaggart to have all the Biblical interpretations; channelers allow the unearthly spirit invading them to state all his or her opinions without objection or discussion. "I don't have any responsibility. I don't even know what the spirit says, because I'm not here during the channelling." The channeler's audience is equally passive, and hears all without asking for evidence. Citizens in the last seven years have acted as if Reagan were a channeler, agreeing with his optimistic opinions on the economy and the poor, even when one had to stumble over the homeless on the sidewalk to get home.

Passivity then entails letting other people do the thinking for you in public areas, but in private areas it can also entail letting other people do the feeling for you. Here we arrive again at a passivity more particular to men; and we notice that some men do ask their wives to do the feeling for them. For example, at a party we meet a computer programmer, rational, unexpressive, impassive, standing next to his empathetic, excitable, fast-talking wife. Such a wife may not only be doing the empathetic feeling for her husband, but also doing his anger. As her marriage with the passive man goes on, she may find herself increasingly angry. We could say that she is angry at his passivity, but she is also carrying and expressing anger that he is not prepared to express.

Of course, it is always possible for a man to ask his wife to do his loving for him as well. That is a more subtle request. In the ordinary course of events, the active male loving that we call courting gradually disappears after marriage, but often nothing substantial takes its place. Maggie Scarf in *Intimate Partners* describes the usual dance that then ensues: the woman desires intimacy, and the man avoids it or resists it — almost. She pursues, but not quite fast enough to catch him, and he flees from intimacy but not quite far enough to break contact. The woman has taken over the active role of pursuing, asking for more conversation, more time together, and the man passively resists. That is a dance which more and more married couples dance. The wife may also take on other active tasks of loving; remembering personal preferences, buying small gifts, noticing times of loneliness, keeping up connections with relatives, taking care of the constant hellos and goodbyes. I am not saying that the woman loves more than the man; I think husband and wife usually have feelings of love roughly equal in intensity and amount. But the passive man will allow the woman to do the expressing, the pursuing, the initiating, the doing.

Such a man may ask his wife to do his parenting for him as well. The father may love the children but not do the parenting. I make a distinction again between love, this time of children, and the intricate tasks involved in loving. As we know, those tasks include setting out helpful rules, reading aloud, encouraging practice on a musical instrument, providing expectations day by day, and year by year, passing on stories of grandparents, teaching children how to solve practical problems with shoelaces and emotions, keeping track of the character of their friends, etc. A man's vigorous activity in one area, earning money or creating art, may not rule out a genuine passivity in some other area. A certain sort of man may even ask his children to do his loving or his feeling for him. Some children pay more attention to the parents' suffering than the parents to do theirs.

What to Do
with Anger and Grief
by John Lee

In my consultations and workshops I see lots of people trying to feel their pain, both anger and grief. I see their feelings struggling up onto their faces and then being swallowed back down. I see people make contact with a feeling, get ready to accept it, maybe even express it for a split second and then run away. They fly away from feeling. That's what I did. That's where I got the title for my book.

I ask these people, "What are you afraid of? If you let yourself really feel your anger or your sadness, what do you think would happen?"

And the answer is always the same. If I've heard it once, I've heard it 300 times.

"John, I don't know. I think if I let myself really go into my anger, I'd tear this house down. I might kill somebody. No one could live with me. I might go crazy."

Or:

"John, if I felt my sadness, I'd drown in tears. I'd never stop crying. My family would leave me. I'd go crazy."

Those answers are wrong. They're backwards. If people don't go into their feelings, their lives will keep on being drowned in tears and murderous fury. The folks they love will be more likely to leave them. They themselves will be more likely to get sick, physically and mentally.

You see, the problem is we don't understand the difference between healthy and unhealthy anger, healthy and unhealthy grief.

Unhealthy anger is anger suppressed, anger denied, anger unfelt.

Unhealthy anger can turn to rage.

And to hate. That's what hate is, according to my friend Dan Jones — anger unexpressed.

I said everybody fears anger, but it isn't anger we fear, it's rage. And with reason. Rage is the ugliest and meanest human emotion. Rage is the father throwing his infant child against the wall and killing her. Rage is the mother scalding her child with boiling water to teach a lesson. Rage is the husband choking the family dog because it sneaked into the house.

Rage is the driver who tailgates you for 10 miles blowing his horn because you cut him off by mistake. Rage is the good church-goer who takes a shotgun and kills five strangers on the street, then blows his own head off.

Rage is awful and has no decent place in normal human relationships. Not at home. Not at work. Not in public.

(Shouts) "Goddamnit! Who left the fucking tricycle in the driveway? Shit!"

That's rage.

(Shouts) "Who left the goddamn pantyhose in the sink?"

So is that.

Now people who get that upset about a tricycle or pantyhose are really acting out an old anger that they weren't able to express.Those of us who grew up in dysfunctional families have been stockpiling anger since childhood. We tried getting angry at Dad when we were four, and we got whipped so hard we learned better. We talked back to Mom at five and were sent to bed without supper for that outburst. We saw we couldn't express our anger safely, so we learned to stuff it in a closet.

Maybe the closet was here, in our neck, so you can hear how full it is from our high-pitched voice. Or maybe the closet was down in our guts, which have so much pain in them they hurt us all the time. Or maybe it was in our sore back or our headachey head.

Wherever we put our closet, it got stuffed full of raw, unexpressed anger. And from time to time some silly thing — the dog coming in with mud on its paws, pantyhose in the sink, a car cutting in front of us on the freeway, our child being 10 minutes late — is going to make the closet door blow off like the lid on a pressure cooker, and the angers of a lifetime are going to pour forth in rage.

When unhealthy, suppressed anger breaks loose; it is rage.

When unhealthy, suppressed grief breaks loose; it is self-pity.

(Sings) "Aw, my baby left me, and I'm gonna stay drunk and lose my job and not shave and smell bad."

"I ain't worth shit. I'm the lowest, meanest, most despicable fart ever drew breath."

"She's a goddess. I'm cowflop."

Rage and self-pity are the classic emotions of the drunk. Some drunks, like my dad, mix them together at the same time. "You goddamn son-of-a-bitch, you're the best friend I ever had."

15

Now why doesn't alcohol help put us in touch with our real feelings? Why aren't rage and self-pity healthy? They're emotions, after all. They break the pattern of control we have been living by.

This is complicated, and I'm not sure I understand it fully. But here's what I think.

Alcohol doesn't help, and rage and self-pity don't relieve us of our pain, because what they express is our false self, not our true one. It's our false self, after all, that's trying to hide from our real anger. It's our false self that denies our grief and pain.

So alcoholics like my dad can get drunk night after night, armoring themselves in their false self, and wake up every morning with that false self broken to pieces, and have to seek the security of their addiction to rebuild the false self, and never come into touch with their real self.

Now, we've still got to answer the question, "What do we do with anger and grief?"

Well, we don't do what we usually do — that's for damn sure.

We don't deny our feelings. We don't bury them. We don't numb them down with TV, food, sex and work.

We don't meditate them away or "transcend" them or "turn them over" before we've experienced them.

We don't mask them under depression or behind a smile.

I had a woman in a group session today who said that when she was five she walked into the living room and her mother kicked her in the stomach. She said that with a smile.

Do you find yourself telling stuff that's deeply painful with a smile on your face? What does the smile say?

It says: "If I smile, I minimize the pain I'm feeling — or I seem to. So I protect me and my mother."

Your mama doesn't need protection. She's a big girl. You can kick her in the stomach, verbally — it's your turn. Or name a pillow after her and punch her out good.

Just imagine the energy it took that woman to tell what she told and smile.

Most of us have so much anger and sadness in us that we spend anywhere from 20 to 80 percent of our disposable energy just keeping them in. And then we wonder why we're tired at the end of the day. Why we weren't more productive at the end of the year.

Let your anger be healthy, clean anger. Not manipulation. Not subterfuge. Not tears.

You've seen that happen — somebody's really angry but they start crying. It's like they can't stay in their anger.

Now there are several reasons for this. Many women can't stay in their anger because they learned nice girls don't get angry. Nice girls eat their anger. Nice boys do, too. They douse the fire of their anger with tears, because tears were more acceptable in their families of origin.

Thank heavens for nice girls and boys. Without them, three-quarters of us therapists would go broke.

Women often turn their anger to tears because they can't afford to get as angry as they feel. If they did, they'd kick their husbands out of the house and be left with the kids and the bills. They cry because crying doesn't cut them off from him as much as anger would.

And there is another reason people cry. They cry because they can't reach their anger. They weren't allowed to as children and now the way is blocked. They cry in frustration. Their real self is cut off from them.

Frustrated people often say the person they're really angry at is themseves. "I keep making the same dumb mistakes in my relationships." "I'm the most godawful codependent in the world." "I've got nobody to blame but myself."

Now this kind of talk is wrong, self-pitying and dangerous.

It's wrong because you certainly do have someone else to blame — whoever taught you the unhealthy patterns you're living by. Do you think I became an alcoholic and learned how to ruin relationships with women all by myself? Nope. My dad was there long before me. And my mom's dad before him.

I need to be appropriately angry at the people and conditions that caused my problem, not only at me.

Now, granted, to set things right, I have to take responsibility for things being wrong. But I mustn't punish myself by thinking that everything's my fault. If I do, guilt and self-pity could immobilize me.

That's the danger when anger is pointed inward at the self — that the self will wilt under the assault. Anger should make us stronger, but if we point it inward it can weaken us.

Now listen closely. I'm going to say this plainly, but you're not going to tell anybody I said it because it sounds a little mystical.

Your emotions. . . my emotions. . . his emotions. . . her emotions don't entirely belong to us. They're not supposed to. They are prompted by things outside us, and we are supposed to express them outside us.

When an emotion comes up in us, what we are meant to do is feel it just as deeply as we can for as long as it works upon us. Then let it go. Express it — literally, push it out — into the universe where it came from.

Trouble starts when we try to keep a negative feeling in us. If we internalize anger, how can we forgive ourselves? If we internalize fear, how can we trust the world? If we internalize grief, what sweetness is there in living?

Feelings aren't supposed to get stuck in us.

But before we can let a feeling go, we have to experience it. And to do this, we have to get in touch with it and feel it.

Now if we can't do this, we need help. We need a safe person and a safe place to work on our feelings — do what I call emotional release work.

I'd like to say that any therapist you go to will be able to help, but this isn't true. Most therapists don't know how to deal with deep anger and deep grief. You say, "I'm sad," and the therapist says, "Yes? Tell me about it." And you go straight to your head, rather than to the grief that's in your body.

It's even worse with anger. Just look at the therapist's counseling room. Smooth desk, pictures, fancy chairs, flowers in breakable vases. You're paying for all that in more ways than one. That's a room people aren't supposed to get angry in.

I went to a therapist who was very good, but she didn't allow anger. She did allow grief, which helped me a lot. She allowed grief because she'd been through grief herself and knew how much it counted. So I could cry and cry without having to intellectualize it.

Which is just what you want to do.

You want to do with your anger and grief what you do with all your feelings. Feel them — feel them as much as you can. Experience them. Then, when you're done, express them and let them pass from you into the world.

When a feeling comes up again, you do the same thing again.

You get rid of your repressed anger and grief the same way you piled them in your closet: one layer at a time.

Or let's change the metaphor. Instead of a closet, let's make your stockpile of feelings a well. You empty the well the same way it fills: drop by drop, dipper by dipper.

Do you ever get to the bottom?

I know I haven't. And I don't know how you'd know if you did. But you reduce the contents and their pressure in you.

Now to do this takes time and patience. And adult children from dysfunctional families aren't patient. Oh, we can wait forever — but we haven't any patience, right?

We want a quick fix. We want a pill that will make our grief and anger go away — snap! like that. We want a spiritual path that will — I think I got this quote from a New Age journal — "Burn our negativity in the white light of the heart chakra."

Ahhh! Burn me, baby!

If it works for you, that's great. It doesn't work for me.

The pain was laid in one layer at a time since we were three, four, five. I believe it has to come out the same way. This is why I favor the Gestalt method of re-experiencing feeling to close old wounds and bio-energetics to discharge the body's blocked energy.

Let me say again what I mean to say in every talk. The way to your feelings is through your body. That's the only place you feel. So, to heal your spirit, you have to start with your body.

One time I had a client, a man of 46. When he was nine, he saw his father go after his mother with a carving knife. He was deeply angry to have watched his father do that and have been too small to do anything about it. He was angry mainly at himself. He shouldn't have been, but telling him this didn't do any good.

I said to him, "Paul, what did you want to do then — when you saw your dad with the knife?"

He said, "I wanted to grab my dad's wrist and make him drop it."

As he said those words, his hands moved in the air — they sort of darted up — and he leaned forward in the chair.

He had been wanting to do something for 37 years. He'd been replaying and replaying in his mind the scene that fueled his anger, but he had never expressed it in his body.

So I suggested we do some psychodrama. I played the dad. I pretended I had a knife, and he went for my wrist and we wrestled as hard as we could, our arms locked together. He was grunting and cursing, till I saw he was completely engaged and I let go.

Right away his body relaxed, and he fell on the floor. He was breathing heavily and so was I. Then, to my surprise, he started laughing. He lay there on the floor and laughed and laughed.

When he was over the conniptions, I said, "Paul, what in God's name was so funny?"

That set him off again! And me, too.

Well, he told me everything was fine. He had finally gotten the pain out. He was laughing because he felt so light. So free.

He said it had seemed a stupid thing to do, the psychodrama, and here it had made him feel so different. He was laughing about that, too.

When people do anger or grief work, their faces get lighter. Look at somebody after he's had a good cry. His face is relaxed and there's a lot of sparkle in his eyes.

Now it's interesting that our culture likes men not to have that sparkle. You know, be like Robert Mitchum. Tall, dark and handsome — that's the phrase. And the darkness is not skin tone. It's moodiness. Sadness. Pain internalized so it clouds the countenance.

Marlon Brando. Jimmy Dean. Robert DeNiro. Mick Jagger. Humphrey Bogart. Al Pacino. Montgomery Clift. I've played them all, trying to impress women.

We need some healthier heroes, that's what it comes down to. We need some men who can surrender their pain and accept joy.

In order to heal, we have to break down the defenses we've put up and feel what we've been hiding from. Come into contact with our real self, and the only way to do it is to lose control.

Now, because we're children of dysfunctional families, we fear the loss of control more than anything. We grew up in situations where there wasn't any healthy control, so we decided about age six that we had to rule the universe. Well, someone with sense had to do it.

But if we're always in control, magic can't happen to us.

The child says, "Mama, this is the most beautiful rock ever, ever. Look at those sparkles." The child is in the magic moment. The child has given control over to the universe, knowing that the universe has endless wonders to show.

If we can't surrender control, we can't see the wonders.

If we can't surrender control, we can't learn to swim — because we fear the water too much.

We can't ride a bicycle — because we fear falling.

We can't fall asleep — because we fear helplessness.

We can't see God in a handful of flowers.

We can't let ourselves have an orgasm.

We can't dance.

We can't cry.

We can't feel.

We can't die.

The Austin paper had an article the other week about a painter, Geoffrey Graham, a gay man who is dying of AIDS. And he said something so beautiful I wrote it down.

"I have no fear of death. It's a natural part of life. I trust the universe enough not to be fearful."

He's surrendered control.

Now we've tried to recapture the uncontrolled, magic moments we knew as children through drugs and alcohol and sex and food. We've used prayer and meditation. And these things have given us little bits of the magic.

My belief is we can get the magic better if we learn to open ourselves to our feelings. When we open ourselves, for a second or two we forget what's around us — just don't care who's watching — and lose control and the need for control. The cries and howls and pain and joy and ecstasy and laughter come up, take us over and pass through us into the universe.

But safely. This loss of control isn't like rage or self-pity — it's safe. The whole time we fought, Paul knew he wasn't fighting with his father.

So it's not like alcohol or drugs or meditation.

We lose control, but we don't lose control.

And we come back from it with the charge gone from our emotions. It's passed back into the universe. Now our anger is clean. We can say "I'm angry" or "I was angry" without frightening other people. Or ourselves.

21

If we need to, after we say, "I'm angry," we can add that dangerous word, because. "I'm angry because we agreed to meet at seven." The person we're speaking to will hear that and understand that our anger comes only from the present event, without a layer of past anger.

The funny thing is, having lost control to get in touch with our feelings, we now have our feelings under control.

The two sets of feelings are different, of course. One is the dirty mound of childhood feelings in our closet. The other is small, clean anger growing out of what's just happened.

So, OK — what do we do with our anger and grief?

First, we feel them. Just as hard and deeply as we can. This sometimes means we have to withdraw from other people. It may mean getting with a safe person to talk to. Someone who will support us, give us reassuring hugs if we need them.

Second, if our feeling is bigger than makes sense, given the event that triggered it, we've got to get in touch with the feelings in our closet, feel them and let them pass.

Third, once the old feelings are over, we return to the world and state flatly what we feel. "I'm sad." "I'm angry." "I feel hurt." Often we don't have to say why — the other person will understand or accept our feeling without knowing the cause. "I was feeling real angry just then, but it's over." "I'm feeling much better, and I'm ready to discuss things with you."

If we have to make a negative judgment on someone, we do it flatly, without demeaning them. "I'm sorry; this isn't working, and I am going to make some changes." "I've decided not to reappoint you. You see the job one way, I see it another. I want to work with someone else." "We've had a good time as lovers. I hope we'll have a good time as friends. I'm very sad to do this, but I want out and I'm getting out."

The frightening passions of anger and grief can be made safe — or anyhow a lot safer.

Fear and Masculinity
by Marvin Allen

I stood naked on the bank and watched the brownish water swirling past, carrying tree limbs and debris in the fast moving current. The boys on the other side of the flooded creek yelled "encouragement" to me. "What's the matter? Chicken? You gettin' yellow? Hey, if we can do it, so can you. Are you a girl, or a queer, or what? Come on, you can do it." I had never been a good swimmer and I wasn't at all sure I could swim across the creek. I was scared, but I knew I had to dive in. I had no choice. In that moment, at 11 years old, the fear of being judged sissy, less than manly, was stronger than my fear of death.

After hesitating long enough to jeopardize my fragile masculinity, I dove into the chilly, muddy creek and immediately began thrashing as hard and fast as I could. Aided by cupfuls of adrenaline that must have been dumped into my fearful body, I managed to make it to the other side — after being carried downstream only a hundred feet or so. My friends congratulated me as they pulled me up through the slimy red mud of the opposite bank. I was cold, shaking, and shaken, but I had passed the test. I was one of them. I belonged. It was an informal ritual of sorts. But like so many of the pseudo-rituals I had volunteered for, it hadn't proven I was a man or ushered me into some higher stage of development. All it proved was, for that moment, I wasn't a sissy, or a girl, or a coward.

Some 20 years later, I stood alone on the bank of a river and idly watched as the current swiftly carried small twigs and water bugs past me. As I watched, I began to remember the scene on the banks of that dirty little creek and how scared I'd been. Once again, I heard the voices calling out for me to dive in. I heard the jeers and threats to my masculinity.

Suddenly I had the urge to dive into the river and swim across, as if to prove I wasn't scared anymore. The truth was, I still wasn't a good swimmer, and I was scared to try the river. I looked at the river for a few minutes and slowly began taking off my clothes. I could feel the sting of the jeers, the threats, and the taunts from my boyhood days as I became determined to quiet them once and for all. Silently, I dove into the water and swam as hard and fast as I could. The river seemed much wider then, as fatigue and then panic caught up with me before I was halfway across. Mustering all my reserves, I pushed down my rising fear and flailed my arms and legs just enough to get to the other side. I crawled out of the current and collapsed on a sand bar a hundred yards downriver from where I dove in. I had almost drowned. Although I felt lucky to be alive, I didn't feel like a conqueror or more manly than before. Instead, I felt tired and ashamed that I had succumbed to fear mid-river. That episode became a kind of turning point for me. As I lay on the sand, I realized how much of my life I'd spent trying to prove some vague notion of masculinity.

As far back as I can remember, I was scared of being called a sissy or a coward. I saw so many unfortunate little boys who somehow didn't measure up to the neighborhood standards of manhood. Perhaps they cried when they were hurt. Maybe they wouldn't fight somebody who obviously could beat them up. Maybe they displayed sensitivity to an animal or another kid being abused. Whatever their transgression, they would be shamed with "sissy," "crybaby," "girl," or "scaredy-cat." I'm not sure who taught them, but the older boys in my neighborhood seemed to know a lot about what boys should and shouldn't do. Boys who didn't follow the rules were shamed and ostracized. It didn't take me long to learn the rules of boyhood.

In much the same way, men are shamed and ostracized for behavior that falls outside the realm of approved masculinity. In virtually every culture that has a strong code of masculinity, shame and guilt are used to enforce that code. In primitive cultures, boys going through initiation were often shamed for being boys and for being so close to their mothers. Women were degraded. Displaying feminine qualities was often unacceptable for boys who would be men. Boys were beaten, humiliated, and scared to increase the power of the rituals. The message was clear: follow the rules or be shamed, dishonored and rejected by the people of the village. The sanction of shame and dishonor was usually enough to keep the men obeying the code, even if it meant risking their very lives.

In our modern military, the technique is very similar. In boot camps across the world, shame, dishonor and fear are used to instill new values and codes of behavior. If a recruit falls behind in the marching, exercising, or whatever, he is immediately shamed in front of the others by being called "sissy," "wimp," "queer," "mama's boy," "pretty girl," or some other slur. Very clearly, the soldier must prove himself to be manly or he is rejected.

Many fraternity houses use hazing techniques that employ shaming and fear. Pledges are called "girls," "sissies," "faggots," and "wimps" until they have successfully undergone the rituals and rites of passage. Only then will they become brothers and belong to the group. Only then will they become real men.

Is it any wonder that we feel such fear about our masculinity? It seems that virtually every male in our culture has internalized those voices that are ready to shame us on a moment's notice if our behavior falls short of real manliness. If we feel weak, hesitant, or fearful, those voices come up to shame us. Is it any wonder that we feel such shame and fear when we don't get it up or keep it up for our sexual partner? Even if the partner says it's perfectly OK, most of us still beat ourselves up with shame and dishonor. Is it any wonder that businessmen jumped out of windows during the market crash in the Depression? They failed in their duty as men. Their fear of shame and dishonor was stronger than their fear of death.

As we attempt to redefine masculinity, it is important that we understand how devastating shame has been. We must create a masculinity that feels so natural and so right that it doesn't require shame and fear to instill it and enforce it. We need a masculinity that is life-affirming and comfortable enough so that we choose it of our own free will. We need to learn that there can be more than one type of masculinity and that we can create a manhood that fits our particular needs and personality.

Finally, we need a masculinity that doesn't flex its muscles by pushing against other people or our planet. We need a manliness that doesn't have to scapegoat or denigrate women, gays, people of color, children, or other men who don't quite measure up to some vague standard. We don't need a masculinity that is so rigid, narrow, heavy and oppressive that shame and fear must be used to coerce men into accepting it. Perhaps then men can wear their manhood with true pride and honor instead of fear and false bravado.

Interview with John Bradshaw
by Bill Bruzy

John Bradshaw. nationally recognized speaker, author and workshop leader, is the author of *Bradshaw On the Family*, *Healing the Shame That Binds You* and *Homecoming*. Through his writing and speaking, Bradshaw has championed the inner child and recovery work.

Bill: When we met briefly in Houston, you said you were becoming interested in men's work and the men's movement. Would you like to talk about that?

John: Yes, I am interested in that. Once I've gotten the family systems stuff out there in a way that I want, then I'd like to really focus more on my own issues as a man and connecting with what other men are doing.

Bill: In your inner child work you talk about "original pain." What do you see that men carry as their original pain? What are men's core issues?

John: There is no question that we probably have more repressed fear and sadness than women often do. It is because our culture has allowed women to cry. It has allowed women to be afraid. We may have been just as afraid and just as sad, but we weren't allowed to be. So I think there is deep abdominal pain in a lot of us. There is also a lot of rage in a lot of us, in a lot of us good guys especially.

I can't believe the level of my rage sometimes, and that it's still there, and still comes up from time to time. You know, I'll be in a car — somebody gets in my way and — I'm this nice guy; I really know how to do that act, but there's a lot of rage. I'll get images of women sometimes, the faces of women, and murderous rage. It's a murderous rage.

It was all those years of taking care of my mother's pain. My dad set me up for it, and I never dealt with any of the anger of that and then I went to be a priest. I don't know about other men, but my suspicion is that a lot of us that conformed have the rage as the deepest part of our original pain.

Bill: Your interest in Jungian work and the shadow self is a popular perspective in men's work.

John: I think it is, and what I am really interested in right now, what I would like to do some more with men, is the soulful kind of thing, the stuff that Hillman has done. I think he's brilliant. What he is saying makes a lot of sense to me — that toxic shame and codependency is a disease of polarization.

The reason shadow work is so important is that it is really the work of balancing polarities. Whereas what often happens is that we get in recovery and we get rigid about recovery.

I see a lot of people sort of doing that. "John Bradshaw does original pain work in his treatment center. That's the only way to go and this is the only way to do it." That's polarization. There are lots of ways to do it. Each one of us will do it our own ways too, and each therapist will do it his own way. So I want to get away from anybody's being a follower of John Bradshaw or making what I do into a system. And I wouldn't want to see that happen with the men's movement. It would become rigid or become systematized, so that you would be shamed for not doing a certain kind of work.

Bill: The issue of leadership is prominent in men's work. Men's dominance in society has been related to patriarchal structures, the hierarchical handling of power. We've all been victimized by that. So we've asked, "How the hell do we do this, and not do it the old way?"

John: Well, I don't know the answer. But the contribution I want to make is that whenever we standardize something we take the soul out of it. We make it one level instead of multi-leveled. So to be soulful may mean to do everything we're doing as long as we all know that it isn't it. It isn't the "right" way. The mythopoetic approach, for instance, has some great values in it, but it isn't the only way. I listen to John Lee. It seems to me he has some of the kind of balance I would like to have. I would want to be careful about anything becoming too much of a standard that everybody has to do. What I tried to do at my treatment center is create a model of non-shaming, non-measuring, which means not standardizing. There are a whole lot of different ways to do our work.

It came up recently with my staff there. They were dealing with Masterson's work on borderlines, a more confronting kind of therapy, thinking that non-shaming model doesn't have that in it. I said, "No, that's a perfectly loving, valid model." Confront somebody when they're copping out, but it can be done in a way that doesn't shame them. It can be done in a way that doesn't measure them or judge them or tell them that there is something wrong with them as a person.

I think the idea of soulfulness is that there are many dimensions, like William James' *Varieties of Religious Experience,* there is a variety of experience in finding your manhood. I think my alcoholic experience was an important experience, standing on bars reciting "Gunga Din" with my shirt off. It was crazy in a lot of ways, but in other ways it wasn't. It was the "wildman."

Bill: How do you see male spirituality, what does that look like to you?

John: I was in a monastery and I used to meditate. We used to sing together. We used to sing what was called the office of the Virgin Mary; it was a Catholic monastery. I came to love that. I came to love that time together singing. We started off and none of us could sing. We were laughing our asses off. It was all very funny. But within four months, we were loving it. There was a community that was built out of it. Each voice was very important for our prayer, our song that we sang together, so there was a camaraderie that was built out of that.

I don't know how to translate that into something modern, but the idea of men meditating together, men praying together, is an attractive idea to me. I think spirituality has been a hard area for men. Only in the Twelve-step programs have I found men who would talk about that comfortably. I would think men's spirituality has to be inward. It has to be something that has community. I went to be a priest because I thought we were going to be a band of men that taught. We were going to be teachers. We were a band of men that came together to teach; one man would be the philosopher, one man would be the mathematician and we would have this community where we shared and we shared knowledge. That never happened. There was a lot of ego and a lot of woundedness and a lot of competitiveness there.

Bill: It's interesting; what you are suggesting is that the model for a truly male spirituality may exist in our own culture. We go off borrowing from Native Americans and Tibetans and try doing things that are very foreign to us, but maybe there are things right here that work as a model for us.

John: I think so. There are some anthropological data on initiation rites — those were rites of indoctrination, rites of literally snapping, where you entered people into the cult. You starved them in the woods and made eerie sounds to scare the shit out of them and break down their ego so you could take over their minds.

. I have some hesitation with that model as a sole model of men coming together. I collect Indian artifacts and love drumming. I think the drumming is more about meditating, about altering consciousness. So you really do have it there. You have men coming together and altering consciousness to get a larger consciousness, a larger sense of community, a larger sense of unity with each other. But I think you're right, we don't have to go to other cultures, completely, to get that.

Bill: Competition is one thing that separates us as men and closely tied to that is the idea of success. We talk about men as success objects and we don't want to do that anymore. So I would like to ask you personally because you are a role model for a lot of men; a lot of people would like to be John Bradshaw when they grow up. How has success affected you? Has it brought you closer to other men or has it intruded between you and other men?

John: Well, I'd say generally it has brought me closer. You can either be a prima donna out of this kind of stuff or you can get a better sense of confidence. What I hope has happened is that I've got a better sense of confidence. It's hard to argue that I am popular. It's hard to argue, when we're selling out every place we go, that people do not want to hear what I'm talking about. My shame voices don't beat me up like they used to, because the data is confronting them. Now, that's good because it gives me a better sense of security about myself.

I feel real close to the men in my life that I've really made an effort to be with. Michael's one of them. I have four guys at home, I have Kip and Mark and then I have Wayne Kritsberg and Pat Karns. John Lee and I really haven't had a chance to build a relationship, but I think we could. I don't just pick them out. It's nice to share with people who are doing what I'm doing because there's a lot of loneliness in this. Now, there's a lot of pain in it because there are a few guys who have envy. It's so clear, it's so ravenous. There is one guy in particular that just goes at me. It's very painful stuff. It's very dishonest stuff because I think it's his jealousy but it comes out as intellectual, he will attack large group work as being very dangerous and I hate that kind of stuff because it's so much bullshit.

This is such an inexact science that you could take anybody's psychology and attack it. We've done, for five years, over half a million people and not had one casualty out of that. But here's a guy that's come along and said that anybody who is doing this is irresponsible and you ought to do it with eight people and one therapist. I just hate that kind of stuff.

So what is it about? I think it's about envy and it's about jealousy and what that's about is about a lack of sense of yourself. Somehow I think we can really build a community of men who really are for each other. You know I say to guys in the field, there are enough people to go around. For God's sake, it just isn't an element of scarcity. But I think that old scarcity gets in there and if you love John Lee you don't love me. That's crazy, because we can have lots of different kinds of leaders. That has been a very painful part to me because I really have a need for camaraderie. I have a need for support. I don't like being alone, even though I did that for a lot of my life. I know that isolation is my greatest danger. When I start isolating, I guarantee you I'm in my shit. I get crazy.

I'm going to talk about this tonight. It's what I call mystification; I go back into my trance, and if I don't have guys to feed off of, like my support group, then I know I probably would be crazy right now. I don't know what would have happened to me.

Bill: Well, I am also interested in your practical experience in the workplace. Men and women are having so much trouble and you have had to deal with so much organization over the years. What works?

John: My belief is that you've got to heal the leaders, you've got to get at the top level. I did Texas General; I was the director of human resources there. I had a quarter-of-a-million-dollar budget and I was putting on weekends and counseling people on the job. But it was not until the top guy went to an ashram in India that a whole different thing happened.

Even though he was giving permission for all of this, he was up in his head with it. He wasn't really doing it, there was still a lot of chauvinism going on. There was a lot of sexual acting out going on. I was doing breakfasts for our seven top guys. They'd be great in the breakfast and then they'd go back and I'd hear them yelling at the secretary or shaming the secretary. So I think it's got to be at the highest level and I think it's got to be people who are working on themselves.

I see the workplace as really needing to be redeemed. It's like what came out recently about American executives and their salaries: Iacocca's $5 million a year is 190 times more than any worker. Then they compared that with Japanese leaders' salaries and they were way, way down.

That's like kings and patriarchs. We still have patriarchs. I know that being on the board of directors of an oil company with stock options... literally, if the stock market hadn't crashed, I'd be an enormously wealthy guy just by being on that board, and for no talent whatsoever. If anybody shouldn't have been on the board of an oil company, it was me. I'd just been in the right place at the right time.

I think we need radical democracy, where everybody has a chance and somehow we're part of these companies we're in. I don't want socialism or communism, but I think there's a social democracy and that's what we've got to strive for. If more and more people will refuse to do the other, and more and more people who have done their work will get into powerful positions, we'll change this sucker around.

We've got the data. Tom Peters is writing books saying what matters most is the quality of your relationship with your people. He's telling us that. He did research, he found out; the best companies care about their people.

But my experience was that if it doesn't come from the top it's useless. The bosses come in like parents and say, "Teach our kids good things. We're going to bring them to church every Sunday while we go play tennis, but we're not going to learn any of this and we don't want to do anything to change." Some of those guys are so in need of redemption, they are terribly in need, walking repressed feelings and passive-aggressive rages. We know it. So we've got to get the recovery movement into the workplace. It's probably the most desperate place there is. There is very little that is soulful there. It's tough for guys to have support groups and then have to go back.

Bill: *If you could diagnose society as a dysfunctional family, what survival roles would you see that have developed for men, and if we start to get healthier, how will that influence society?*

John: I think that society is patriarchal, and what we are in right now is this whole anti-patriarchal movement that began with civil disobedience. The gay rights movement was part of it; the women's movement was part of it. The recovery movement is really fighting the oppression of the child. That's what we've been fighting for, the adult child.

Maria Montessori in 1920 said there is not a group of people that has ever been so oppressed as the children. No slave was ever more the property of his master than a child is of his parents. Think of patriarchal rules where you own your children and you crush their will at an early age. The one thing patriarchs hated was willfulness in children.

Nuremberg is the end of an era. That is, all these movements began after Nuremberg. But we still have patriarchal politics, we still have Bush and Dukakis and those guys standing up there thinking that if they bring their families on the stage, we'll think they're a wonderful family and if they say "God," everything is OK.

These are not family people. I was with the daughter of one of the prominent people in Bush's cabinet. She was out in California, she's in recovery, she's been six years in recovery. She was talking about how horrible it was to live with her dad and her mom. Her dad is one of the great men in the world right now.

So I think we have "boy" psychology. Look at all of the politicians who are acting out, look at all the preachers who are acting out. All these so-called leaders in our culture are really little boys in a lot of ways, and little boys who were set up to take care of their mothers' wounds and are acting out. You know, there are a lot of "flying boys" in our society who are in leadership roles. So if we start changing the way men are, if men refuse to sort of do that overly macho thing; in Houston, Texas, right now, they're hijacking cars. It's like old stagecoach robberies. You drive up and somebody grabs your car. So everybody's thinking about getting a gun. It's like the old west again, where you carry a gun to protect yourself.

This is distorted masculinity. Gangs are distorted masculinity. The only thing I know to do is what I can do, which is to own myself, to be as whole as I can possibly be, to be willing to be honest with other men and to try to create a bond where we work on empowering each other.

The guys in my treatment center have all been empowered. They'll tell you they've been empowered by our relationship. Nothing is more important to me, really, than that I am an instrument of empowerment for my friends. Hopefully then, someone is an instrument of empowerment for me.

Bill: Is that mentoring, what you are doing?

John: We have to mentor each other to some degree. We need to help each other, because a lot of times we just don't know what to do. Hope is mutual. It is partly imagining with somebody, being there for them and imagining something that they can't imagine.

I think when we get stuck we get mystified, we get in a trance and we really can't see beyond that trance. That's the nature of a trance. It's a mental fixation.

So we really do need each other and we need each others' point of view and we need each others' imagination. But you've got to come in with the feeling that I'm safe here, that it's a non-shaming environment. Now, I don't think that we will ever be able to create that perfectly, because we're all too wounded.

It's like my shit's going to get in the way some of the time. I don't know, I think we have to keep talking, we have to keep interacting. We have to keep in community.

What happens to me when I get out of community, the trances that get set up with me and my defenses as a child, they're characterized by holding my breath and by going internal. You go self-to-self, rather than self-to-other. So I walked around in an alcoholic, Seconal™, Toulenol™, Nembutal™ trance for all these years, self-to-self.

Going to a meeting is self to other. It is the trance-breaker. The second I'm looking you in the eyes, I'm breaking the trance in some way. I know that nothing is more important to me than this support group I've got, because we sit down at 1 o'clock at my house or George's office, or wherever, and we share where we are and we get feedback. One guy came in there Monday and he was just crazy. He'd been all involved with his family. It was so clear to me how he was back in the trance.

So you sit there and you talk and you get feedback, feeling feedback; we don't do crosstalk, or if I do I try to own it as my stuff. That's a very healing thing to have. I know we've got to have that, we've got to have some kind of community support from each other where we can talk and we can look each other in the eyes, rather than getting isolated. I think the whole style for men in the past has been isolation.

Bill: So is that how you've learned to love yourself as a man, through your group, through this interaction with other guys?

John: Well I think it's a big help. It's that whole idea of "flying boys," where you take care of your mother's wound. I went to the monastery. That's one way to deal with my sexuality, to give my sexuality to God and to Mary Holy Mother.

When I came out, of course, I got really wild and crazy and I always went to women to get fixed. I went to women for nurturing.

I find there is a different strength in having men support me and say "I love you" and having men really call me to myself. Robert Johnson said it recently. It is a lot easier to get into your shadow and know that you're a bum. It's a lot harder to realize that you really have some nobility about you. That's what those guys do to me. That'll get me into tears in about two seconds when they start focusing on "you know, you're really a good man." That's the stuff that just takes my breath away.

My trance was that I wasn't a good man. My mother was an untreated incest victim. She dumped all that contempt and sexualized rage on me. My fantasies were about older women dominating me. So it's been really important for me to feel like a man, having other men value me, and be vulnerable with me and tell me tender things. That's been really important for me.

For me, the way I would want to go in the men's movement is along those lines. I hear John Lee talking about that, too. The mythopoetic has a camaraderie in it and I could do that as a trip. But I could see getting into competitiveness about that. I don't want to discount it at all, but I just want to say that my way would be more of a tender sharing with men.

I don't know whether I agree with Bly that we're soft males. I don't know, really, what that means. I know that when I was drinking I was a wild, crazy, fighting maniac. I did do a lot of wild, crazy stuff and took a lot of risks.

Somehow I don't feel that I need to develop that part of me. I feel like I need to develop the more tender, vulnerable part of me that's scared so much.

Bill: *That's very beautiful.*

John: I'm real grateful that you all are doing what you're doing in that you're carrying the ball right now. I really want you to hear that. It's a really fine work and I think it's going to help a lot of men, it's helping a lot of men.

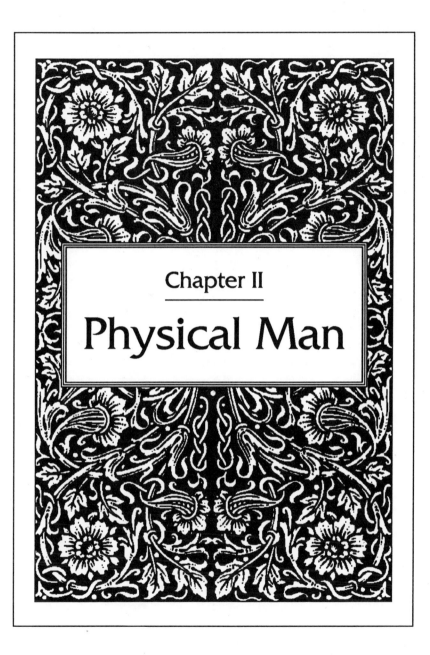

Chapter II
Physical Man

Salute to the Morning
by Jim Hagen

For 25 years, I have been meeting the same friend to hike and camp, usually in the Berkshires in western Massachusetts an equal distance from our two homes, New York City for me, and Boston for George. We usually do this two or three times a year. One major concession to our modern tastes and growing years is when we hike in the winter, we treat ourselves to the comfort of a warm motel room.

On a trip this past winter at six in the morning, the raucous sound of the alarm clock went off, an alarm left set by some previous traveler. I leaped from the bed, naked, lurched for the clock and slammed it, twisted it and finally shut the damn thing off. Only then did I sense my nakedness and my hardness. I had been seen saluting the morning.

Whether it is from pressure on the kidneys (thus the expression "piss-hard-on") or left over arousal from a forgotten but juicy dream makes little difference to most of us. What does matter is that the day often begins with the half awake/half asleep state that eases us into consciousness with the affirmation of a hard-on.

And it is affirming. That's why I like to prolong the moment, roll over on my back and slide my hand down my belly to grab tight as I doze on. It is affirming just to hold it first thing in the morning, knowing that I don't have to do anything with it, but just enjoy it for itself. To enjoy myself for myself. Just as the little lights on a dashboard light up when I first turn the key to let me know that all systems are working, it's comforting to hold on first thing in the morning, knowing that even though the rest of me is still asleep, there is at least one part of me that is up and ready. I know I am not my penis, yet what a wonderful way to start the day, a great "Yes!" to life, a standing to attention, a salute to me and to the day, whatever it brings.

Yet as affirming as a morning hard-on can be, it's embarrassing — something to be hidden.

Even D.H. Lawrence, that celebrator of sex, catches the ambiguity in *Lady Chatterly's Lover*, where there is an early morning scene after Connie and Mellors have spent the night together. It's 5:30, the sun is coming up and she asks him to open the curtains. By this time in the book the aristocratic women and the rough gameskeeper have broken through the class barriers that had separated them and now have a new freedom in an uninhibited sensuality. Mellors gets out of bed, goes to the window and opens the curtain letting in a warm beam of golden light. But then he freezes. "He was ashamed to turn to her, because of his aroused nakedness." He grabs his shirt to cover himself, but she says, "No . . . let me see you." So he drops the shirt and stands still, looking towards her. Mellors, like countless others of us, starts the day with mixed feelings: he salutes the morning with an erection, but is embarrassed.

That's how I felt that morning with my friend, going for the clock. The only thing said about it later was George's comment: "You were really standing right up this morning when you went for the alarm." He knows me better than almost anyone except my wife. There is nothing to hide from him. Yet it's only when caught unawares, when I am unconscious of my body and going for the clock, that I can be so uninhibited.

It's strange how I want to be covered, even with such a good friend. Under the safety of the covers, in the darkness of my own private world, I can be uninhibited, strong, hard, affirmed. I can be myself, human and natural. But out from under the covers, seen for how I am, whether hard or soft, my natural state becomes the source of embarrassment, a sign of weakness. To be human, to let my naturalness show is to be vulnerable. And for me, something to be quickly covered again.

I wonder if being seen with a morning hard-on is for a man what being seen without makeup is for some women: there you are, letting nature take its course, letting it have its say, but feeling somehow you have to apologize for the state you are in.

A morning hard-on is an important male experience. It stands (pardon the pun) for what we often experience as males, not only first thing in the morning, but all day long: hardness, readiness, being up, on top, firm, powerful, potent. Like the five-year-old son of a friend of mine who says for all of us as he pointed to his erect penis: "Look Daddy, I can be big, too."

It is comforting to have attached to my body a potent reminder of power. But there is the threat.

Is the power I feel in the morning going to be there when I need it during the day? The threat is I will be soft when a situation comes along that demands (at least in my mind) hardness; that I will shrink instead of standing tall. The fear is, in a word, of being impotent.

And then on the mornings when I wake up soft, even in the haze that clouds my brain, I can't help but think that I have missed something. And sometimes I make the first action of the day some strokes to get hard for the affirmation I seem to want and need. But softness is as much a salute to life as hardness. It is as much of who I am, just as much of the male experience.

It is ironic that the side of me that I hide under the covers, my hardness, is the very side of my personality that I think others demand of me in order to get through the day. I have to be upstanding at the office, firmly aggressive while driving the car across the 59th Street Bridge, hard and forceful getting through the door on the subway at rush hour. But my softness, which I feel free to show, for example, as I walk naked in the shower at the YMCA after a game of racquetball, once outside and dealing with people, is the side of me that goes under the blankets. I find I am hesitant to show my gentle side, to let people see me when I'm down. Hide the hard-on but show my firmness. Be free to be seen with a soft penis, but never let softness show.

My salute to the morning makes its point: being human can be affirming and threatening, and sometimes both at the same time.

Touching the Masculine Soul
by Barry Cooney

My father was not a violent man, but his temperament always vacillated between contained rage and emotional disenchantment. Around him there was little room for outward displays of emotion. Looking back on my formative years, it's difficult to remember many instances of being held or touched by my father. I didn't realize it at the time, but I was starving for male affection. On those rare occasions when I felt my dad squeeze my shoulder in a loving, supportive way, my body would surge with ecstasy and delight. Recently, it has become apparent how vital it is for men to be touched by other men. Recognition by the "Father-King" provides emotional sustenance. Without it, we are less complete as males.

Latin, Mediterranean and Eastern European cultures seem to have a deeper understanding of this need. Anyone who has visited South America has witnessed the "abrazo," or hug, that takes place when two or more male friends meet. I recall with stunning vividness my first weeks in Budapest as a graduate research assistant. There in the University Square, men of all ages walked arm in arm. At first, I was a little confused by their behavior. Gradually, I realized that this display of warmth and affection was not sexual, but arose from a deeper awareness of the need for males to bond with other males. Returning to the United States, I was shocked to see men recoiling from one another in crowded elevators or hands being quickly removed as soon as the shake exceeded its customary two-second limit.

Is it any wonder why men in North America remain untrusting and self-centered, or why we bare our souls more openly to women than to our fellow brothers?

The taboos against males' touching males in our society can be traced back to the thinking of our Puritan fathers. Their philosophy is one rooted in hard work, skepticism and sin, with little time left over for anything else. According to their model, emotional expression is always suspect. (Life, it seemed, was serious business.) The same is true in lovemaking, which was supposed to be carried out as a joyless procedure for procreating the species.

Prior to the men's movement of the last decade, signs of male affection were exhibited mostly by gay men. For those of us who took pride in being super studs, demonstrating physical affection to another male was definitely forbidden. However, in my case, the need to touch and be touched by a man was so strong, that I knew I needed to search for someone who might be sympathetic to my plight.

I didn't have long to wait. The opportunity arose during my first job as a therapist in a large, East Coast teaching hospital. One of the chief psychiatrists (let's call him Bob), approached me after a staff meeting. Would I have dinner with him? "Sure, I'd be delighted," I remember saying. It was my suspicion that Bob was gay. However, the thought of Bob's homosexuality or of his invitation to dinner was in no way threatening to my sense of masculinity. To me, Bob was a sensitive, extremely bright and highly cultured human being, a person whom I'd like to have as a friend.

We strolled along narrow cobblestone streets, talking about art and music. After a while, we stopped in front of an enormous, carved, mahogany door. Turning abruptly, Bob struck the gold knocker, giving it two sharp taps. The door swung open and we were greeted by a tall, husky waiter with a huge handlebar moustache. Suddenly I found myself sitting in one of the city's most exclusive gay restaurants.

As we casually ate our superb meal, Bob talked freely about his homosexuality. He was the son of an alcoholic father who had abandoned both his mother and him when Bob was only nine years old. He developed a serious interest in men only a few years after that incident.

At one point during dinner, in the middle of a particularly painful part of his story, Bob spontaneously reached over and held my hand. It seemed an appropriate gesture, given the situation. I remember thinking how unusual it would have been for any of my male friends or family members to extend themselves in such a manner. (The only exception to this rule came at Irish funerals of distant relatives. Occasionally, amidst the arguing and crying, one could observe two or three men locked in a tearful, drunken embrace.)

As a result of our dinner meeting, Bob and I developed a close friendship. While he recognized that I was a "hard-core hetero," Bob was also aware of my own sensitivity. During the years we knew each other, I could always count on him for a warm hug at the end of a stressful day, or after my marriage ended, a needed shoulder to grasp when the pain became unbearable.

It's clear that my involvement with this gay psychiatrist was primarily therapeutic in nature. Being able to share the intimacy of touch,

41

in many ways satisfied my tremendous emotional hunger for male affection. I felt stronger and more complete because of that friendship. Males who are denied appropriate physical affection with other males while growing up become people who never actually mature. In fact, many men who are so denied will strongly repress their need for manly affection. You can see these men at any football game or boxing match. They seem to thrive on the violent aspects of male contact, while distancing themselves from any form of intimacy.

At a recent workshop for men that I conducted in Toronto, Canada, I was working with a group of males whose ages ranged from 25 to 69 years. As is the case with most gatherings of this nature, there was a tremendous recounting of stories involving physically or emotionally absent fathers. As the workshop progressed and we moved through exercises that allowed us to express our emotions openly, it was clear that the supportive hugs and embraces being exchanged represented feelings that had been held in check for many years. For the men older than 50, listening to younger males speak of their need for the "fatherly embrace" seemed to break open their protective shells, allowing them to experience the deep healing that takes place when males begin to bond emotionally with other males.

One powerful aspect of the men's movement is its emphasis on this form of bonding. When men are allowed to freely experience the love and support of other men, they begin to question competition in our society. This questioning engenders a willingness to engage in more service projects and activities whose aim is to nurture and protect the planet.

Thus, the "feeling man" becomes fully initiated into manhood and carries out his role as a protector, healer and teacher to other men. He enters, to paraphrase the late Joseph Campbell, a transpersonal state of consciousness in which service to his selfish ego is replaced by a desire to lend his energy and support to the greater good of humankind. Here lies the power of the New Masculine Soul. It all begins with an embrace.

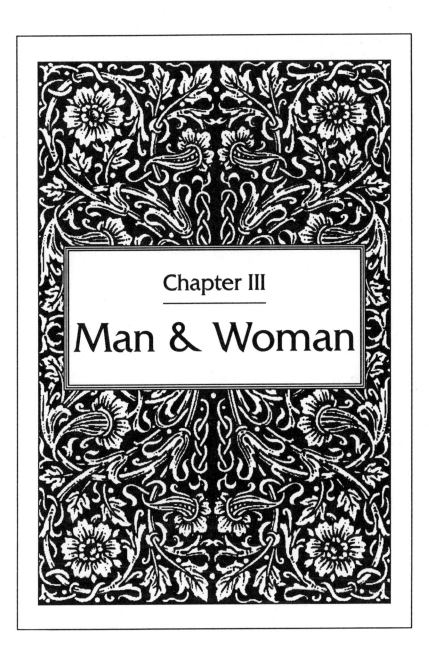

Chapter III

Man & Woman

Letting Go of Being Alone
by John Lee

Lucy and I moved in and out of intimacy like two kids trying to enter a cold-water bath or water too hot to touch. But there was so much good stuff that I wanted to believe she was the one.

One night she and I were arguing about some insignificant something and I got up, put on a pair of shorts, and stomped to the front porch. I looked into the darkness and then at the pattern that I was living out.

I thought to myself, "My God, how many times have you been right here before?" The answer was, "Hundreds." I thought, "It's time to break some old patterns and see what happens."

My pattern is to leave. According to my pattern I would go back in the house, get dressed, tell whoever was lying in the dark that I was going for a drive and come back in several hours and stuff whatever emotions might be trying to surface. At that moment I ran the pattern through my mind's eye. I decided to do something immediately, anything as long as it was different. So I got up and moved past the fears and went back to bed and said, "Please hold me." Lucy did, and I cried and told her I was hurting. The next morning, I felt like I'd punched a hole in a lifelong pattern that had ruled me. She then felt free enough to break into tears herself and asked me to hold her as she went into her own painful place. We came close and we managed to tear down some walls.

Breaking patterns is hard. First they have to be identified, but identification won't break them. We have to not only see what they are but what we get out of them. There is no pattern that we've ever adopted that does not get us something. When it no longer serves us, we stop doing it. First we name it, then see where it came from, what it gets us and then go against it. Sounds easy, doesn't it? Well, we all know it's not easy. Here's one reason why.

I asked a client of mine who was describing the patterns he and his wife have around intimacy, "Richard, what do you get out of those patterns?"

"Nothing but pain," he responded.

"Bullshit, you get something, or you wouldn't do them," I responded. Richard looked at me, surprised at my language or my readiness to confront him. "I don't get anything but the same old thing."

"Bingo!" I said. "The same old thing. Listen to what you're saying."

I asked Richard to tell me how the pattern performs its magic. In a nutshell, what he said was this: "She'll do this and I'll do this, and then she'll do this and I'll wait a few days and say this, and then she'll respond and then everything will be OK until next time."

What Richard said for all of us who rely on patterns is that as long as we let them run us, we know exactly how things are going to turn out — the same way they always do. Knowing how this will turn out is worth so much to the many of us who are control freaks. It gives us a sense of order, even if it hurts like hell. Most of us prefer the known to the unknown, and any time we try to go against or break a pattern, we plunge headlong into the unknown where all kinds of things await us. That's scary, so we stay with the familiar, even though it cripples us in relationships.

When I got up and went from the porch and out of the pattern, I made a journey into the mystery, into the magic of the moment, and I was terrified. Would Lucy reject me? Laugh at me? Leave me? Love me?

A long time ago, a particular response to a particular situation worked for us, saved us and allowed us to survive something. Responses are usually only good for one event, but we turn them into patterns that almost never work the way they did the first time.

Each time we go against a pattern that has shielded us from the raw opportunities of the moment, we create an opportunity for change for all those involved. If I stop doing what I've always been counted on by others to do, they have to stop what they've always done as well. If I shift, the other person has no one to bounce off of. Thus they are left either to discover something else to do or go find someone else who will enable them to play out their ancient pattern. And many of us are deathly afraid that they'll do just that — leave us and go find someone else who will match their patterns the way one or both of their parents did.

In my family of origin, I never saw much letting go or detaching. What I saw was someone, my dad or mom, threatening to leave or trying to control the other through threats, manipulation and domination. My mom's love was off the mark as much as my alcoholic father's. Neither could let go of the other or us children. She was unconsciously dependent on him and his drinking. She got things from him which she didn't think she could live without. He took care of her financially, and she got to take care of him physically, emotionally and spiritually and in the process appear to be the long-suffering devoted wife.

Mom could not let go of Dad and detach, and Dad couldn't let go of Mom. Neither could hear their still small inner voice that must have whispered, perhaps screamed, that they should love each other enough to set the other free. Instead, they clung to each other out of desperation, rather than loving devotion. Mom, who never learned to swim, clung to Dad like a life preserver in a sea made of tears, but the life preserver offered little buoyancy.

Somewhere, somehow, in spite of all this I learned to listen to that voice inside me. Not all the time, but a good portion of the time. I could trust that voice to guide me the way it did when it told me to go to the place where I would meet Laural.

When Laural and I first parted, now over four years ago, I asked her why she was leaving. "John, you didn't love me the way I needed. And you didn't teach me a whole lot. But one thing you did do. By listening to your own inner voice, you showed me that I must listen to my own. For that I thank you."

"What did your inner voice tell you to do?" I asked, already knowing the answer.

"It said I had to leave you."

"That inner voice," I said with a smile, because I was happy for her and glad she got something from me besides pain, "that inner voice — you can't go around trusting just any old inner voice. Who told you that stuff? Your real inner voice would say, 'Stay, Stay, Stay!' "

We both laughed for the first time in months. "Well, if your voice said go, I guess that's what you'd better do. You think you'll ever come back?" Tears began falling. "I will if my inner voice tells me to." She hugged me and I knew then she was gone, though it would take years to accept.

She loved herself and me enough to let go. I've been trying to learn how for a long time. But I began practicing with Lucy and I did fairly well. One of the ways I did this was to begin grieving and releasing the sadness and anger around what I already knew to be an ill-fated future for us as a couple. After she'd go back to Mississippi or I'd leave her there, I'd usually spend quite a bit of time in tears. When I got to somewhere safe, I would scream and yell and pound out my anger. It was in this form of letting go I could release her more honestly and deeply.

But a curious thing always happened for a while. The more I'd let her go, the more she could and would be there. I see now that when someone fears intimacy, possession and abandonment, the more room they need to feel safe and hold on. The result would be her feeling forced to leave. It seems the very thing we're afraid of the most is the thing that is guaranteed to happen, since most of our actions are directed and patterned to get the results we say we don't want. I didn't want Laural or Lucy to leave, and yet leaving was what I had always known. Staying I didn't know and didn't trust. I only knew how to be alone. The truth is that clinging and holding onto anything in life is just the opposite of what life demands — letting go. I really started my training with a woman who was as hard to hold as the wind.

The Nice Guy, Part 1
by Marvin Allen

Demographics, absent or dysfunctional fathers, and the women's movement have combined to usher in the era of the Pleasing Male. Fathers, if they live at home, preoccupied with work, fatigue, or addictions have little time for sons hungry for masculine attention. Little boys, ignored or abused by their fathers, must turn back to the mother for safety, nurturing and validation. The love, acceptance, mirroring and identity formation that normally should come from both parents too often comes only from the mother. She becomes too important to us as little boys. For many of us, pleasing her becomes a means of survival and a way of life.

The women's movement has made most men keenly aware of the destructive nature of the old, distorted image of man as macho robot. Many men are almost apologetic for being males. Some men, raised by women, uncomfortable around males, have learned to reject everything that sounds like machismo in their desire for acceptance. For a growing number of adult men, acceptance and validation come only from females. What we learned as boys, we remember as men. We started out pleasing our mothers, and we end up pleasing our wives or girlfriends.

As a kid, I was your typical fun-loving, get-in-trouble little boy. I liked to play catch with my brother, hide-and-seek with the neighbors' kids, and I even played jacks with my big sister. I studied nature by dropping ants down "doodle bug" holes, or pulling wings off butterflies. I satisfied my hunting instincts by catching sparrows in mousetraps and shooting roaches with a rubber-band gun. My sister had this strange affinity for creatures of all kinds, and so she didn't appreciate my talents as a young hunter. Other than that, we seemed to get along very well. In fact, I got along fairly well with everyone in my family and in my neighborhood, except my dad. As a very young child, I remember being happy and even fairly well adjusted.

Gradually, things began to change for me. My father, himself a victim of an abusive family, didn't seem to care much for marriage or children. He mostly read his newspaper or watched television. If he wasn't doing one or the other, he was usually irritable, frustrated, or downright angry. Dad couldn't contain anger very well, so when he got mad, he would strike out at anyone or anything close to him. If one of us kids were too close, he would use his belt to express his feelings.

When I look back, I wonder why my mother didn't intervene more often on our behalf. Although memory reveals her to be nurturing and loving, perhaps she just seems that way in comparison to him. My dad was sort of afraid of her and never laid a hand on her and rarely even yelled at her. She could have stopped him from mistreating us children, but she didn't. I'm still working to understand that.

As a little boy, however, I clung to her as a safe harbor because she didn't hurt me like Dad did. I needed to believe in somebody. I needed to believe that somebody would love and protect me. I guess she won that job pretty much by default.

I gradually learned that if I did certain things to please her, my mother would be more responsive to me. She would smile more and she would talk to me. If I put up my toys, she would tell me what a good little boy I was. That felt really good to me. Later, I learned to sweep the floors and anticipate her moods and to cheer her when she was down or placate her when she was frustrated. At the time, I thought I was being good because I loved her so much. Now I know I did those things because I needed so much for her to love me.

It wasn't easy trying to please my mother. She was often depressed or distressed from living with my dad. She also came from a rather "colorful" family and had strange moods of her own. Not all of my pleasing attempts worked to gain her favor. Caught in one of her darker moods, she often ignored or criticized my childish efforts to please. Yet her occasional smile or pleasant response seemed to create in me an indelibly reinforced pattern of pleasing behavior.

It was a short step to go from pleasing Mother to pleasing my elementary school teachers. I watched them carefully and learned what behaviors pleased them and what made them mad. Being the teacher's pet came quite naturally for me. I must admit that an occasional burst of pent-up exuberance forced me to talk too much or to pull someone's ponytail. Those moments of indiscretion showed up as X's in conduct on my report card and became grounds for disapproval and shame from my parents. Because exuberance wasn't something that people seemed to appreciate, I pretty much learned to overcome it. That is, until the last day of class in the sixth grade. After class that afternoon, I just couldn't help myself. In an ecstatic gesture that surely reflected my truest feelings about lower education, I threw all my school papers into the air and watched the wind scatter them over the school yard. Unfortunately, my art teacher, a modern-day version of Attila the Hun, saw me from her window. Her telephone call arrived at my home before I did. My mother had gone from a dark mood into a black hole. That wretched human failing, exuberance, had left its mark on me yet again. That evening, coupled with the embarrassment of adolescence and the responsibility of adulthood, pretty well put the lid on exuberance for me, except maybe where girls were concerned.

As a teen-ager I learned that pleasing girls got me even more goodies than pleasing teachers. Although I had been a reluctant Baptist for years, I never had the faintest idea what heaven was like until I kissed my first girl. And it was so easy! All I had to do was be nice to the girls and please them. They responded by telling me how sweet I was and what a good person I was. I'd been looking for that kind of talk for a long time. Not only did they say nice things to me, but they would hold me and kiss me as well. I felt like a part of me had finally come home.

Another short, quick step found me, at 19, pleasing a wife and baby girl. In our early days of courtship, my wife had said jokingly, "You're so nice, it's just unreal." Little did we both know how true that statement was. Slowly, yet inexorably, my rage, my shame and my fears began to rear their ugly heads. Dark, angry moods began to interfere with my pleasing behavior. Although my wife was loving and caring enough, I began to resent her and the baby. I felt emotionally undernourished and I blamed them for it. I gradually reached the point where I was either withdrawn and passive or I was inappropriately angry. Kind of sounds like dear old Dad, doesn't it? Finally, I left my family so I could be with people who could really appreciate what I had to offer.

Once again, I felt like I had reached the very gates of heaven. My hard work and pleasing behavior rewarded me with a flourishing business and a flock of girlfriends. I had more strokes, more affection and more money than I knew what to do with. Yet, with all that, in rare, quiet moments, I felt painfully alone, restless and empty. Although I didn't know what I was afraid of, I felt scared most of the time. Those old skeletons of grief and fear and rage were rattling around, trying to get out. To me, they were just part of that same old horror movie that played throughout my childhood. I'd seen enough of it, and I just wanted to get on with my own life as a grown-up. I managed to keep those old skeletons at bay by changing girlfriends and working even harder. With boundless energy, vigilance and sheer force of will, I kept reaching up and pulling the heavens down around me. The problem was that every time I turned my head or took a nap, heaven left and I found myself in a kind of hell. Somehow, I knew life wasn't supposed to be this way. I just didn't know what to do to change it. After years of this kind of "life," numbing fatigue, despair and therapy finally slowed me down enough to start catching up with myself.

Of all the dysfunctional patterns I created out of my childhood, I think workaholism and hyper-pleasing have been the most insidious and the most destructive. For me, pleasing and workaholism have been practically synonymous with each other. The more I worked, the more it pleased those receiving my products and services. The more they were pleased, the more money I could make. The more money I made, the more the people around me would be pleased. The more I could please the people around me, the more I could please that internal critic inside of me. Somehow, however, my internal critic was never quite convinced of my worthiness. It seemed to keep a constant vigil on my behavior, my feelings and even my thoughts, duly noting and recording all substandard performance. My critic met successes with questions like "yes, you did this, but can you do this other thing?" It seems in retrospect that the critic was infinitely more interested in my flaws and failures than in my successes. The pleasing man, it appears, is never pleased with himself.

The Nice Guy, Part 2

by Marvin Allen

On Monday, George and his 10-year-old son, Danny, decided to spend the coming weekend fishing and camping. As the week progressed, they talked and planned excitedly. On Friday morning, however, George's wife, Mary, complained that she was tired and wasn't sure what she would do with herself during the weekend. When George invited her once again to go along on the camping trip, Mary replied, "Mosquitoes, snakes and dead fish don't sound like much fun to me."

Friday afternoon when Danny arrived home from school, George told him that the timing just wasn't right for the fishing trip. There were just too many things to do around the house. Growing accustomed to this sort of disappointment, Danny held back the tears and said, "That's OK, Dad. I understand. We'll do it next time, OK?"

"Yeah, son. We'll do it next time for sure. I promise," George answered sincerely.

George spent the weekend mowing the yard, cleaning up around the house and spending a lot of time with Mary, who seemed to be feeling much better.

On the surface, one might view this scenario as a demonstration of George's love for his wife. If we could peek below the surface, however, we might see a different picture. Perhaps George's pleasing behavior is neither a gift to Mary, nor is it a reflection of his caring and concern. Instead, George's actions may be an unconscious attempt to keep Mary from leaving him. This abandonment anxiety, lurking in the shadows of his mind, may influence George to automatically acquiesce to Mary's perceived needs, while ignoring or neglecting his own needs and those of his son.

Like George, millions of contemporary males have become confused about the issue of pleasing the women or lovers in their lives. This Nice Guy syndrome can take many forms. Sometimes a man may spend a month's salary on Christmas presents for his beloved. Or he may go to endless social functions or get-togethers with the in-laws just to be accommodating. He may even eat her broccoli, or go to restaurants or movies he would otherwise avoid. Nice Guys often turn into the Handyman. This poor guy lives to fix anything that appears broken: her feelings, her washing machine, even her poodle's broken leg. If he's not fixing things, he feels anxious and unworthy.

For most of us, this Nice Guy syndrome started in early childhood. Because our fathers weren't there for us, either emotionally or physically, many of us had to rely too much on our mothers for psychological survival. Considering our alternatives, pleasing our mothers became our most intelligent behavior option. If the mother's needs are not being met by her husband, a support system, or by herself, then she may become dependent upon the child to meet her needs. She conditions and reinforces the child by approving and "loving" him when he pleases her, and disapproves, withdraws, or punishes him when he doesn't. As small boys, many of us learned to "take care of" our mothers and their feelings so they could take care of us. To take care of them, we had to disregard our own needs and feelings.

In our egocentric, little-boy minds, mother's love and sometimes her very survival seemed to depend on our behavior. This kind of early codependent relationship leaves us with an insecure attachment to our mothers. We can't just take her love and presence. We often come to believe that unless we behave a certain way, mother may not only stop loving us, but may abandon us, as well. Behaving a certain way usually includes stuffing our feelings, such as anger, fear and sadness. If mother's fighting her own fear, the last thing she needs is for us to be frightened. If she's full of anger and rage, she'll have a hard time dealing with our own anger. To keep mother from abandoning us, we learn to abandon ourselves.

If we developed an insecure attachment with our mother, the chances are good we'll develop the same kind of attachment to our lovers, whether they're men or women. This means we get to continue the process we learned so well as boys. At 40 or 50 years old, many of us are still trying to keep mama from leaving us by pleasing our wives and suppressing our feelings. Just below the surface, there's the fear that she could leave at any time. To keep that fear at bay, we're often willing (even eager) to abandon ourselves, our friends and our children. Considering the price we pay, is it any wonder that beneath our pleasing smiles is often a smoldering anger that approaches rage? Is it any wonder that, mixed with our pleasing ways, is a certain amount of controlling, possessive, obsessive behavior? How can we believe she loves us for ourselves when we gave up ourselves to please her? Isn't our underlying belief that she loves us for our pleasing behavior?

This, of course, points us toward the supreme irony of the Nice Guy syndrome. We have a core belief that, to be loved, we must hide our real selves and feelings while we please and perform. Yet, just below the surface is the knowledge that they "love" us precisely for our performance and not for ourselves. We are conditioned to please, and yet the more we automatically please, the less chance we have to feel truly loved. If we please to be loved, we can never feel loved. It is like buying love. In this case, the price we too often have paid is the diminishment of our very souls. Compromising our souls to keep from being abandoned might have been a bargain when we were three years old, but it's a tragic, unnecessary waste at 40.

Breaking out of the Nice Guy syndrome can be complex and difficult. The first step out of the morass is to own what we are doing. As we become aware of the process, we need to watch ourselves in action without judging our behavior. We need to develop gradually that inner taste that distinguishes between pleasing to be loved and pleasing because we love.

As we own what we are doing, we also need to own our feelings of anger, grief and fear. Those around us who have come to expect our pleasing behavior may experience our real feelings as rejecting or threatening. We must learn to express our difficult emotions appropriately, to avoid intimidating or shutting down those friends and lovers. Remember, when we begin to express our anger, rage from our childhood may come up with it, causing our feelings to seem inappropriate for the present context. We must get out the rage and then practice appropriate expression of anger until it becomes natural.

As we begin to own and express our feelings, we get to know ourselves in a new and refreshing way. Our feelings become an important source of information about who we are and what we need and desire. With our appropriately felt and expressed anger comes the ability to assert our needs and to protect our limits and boundaries. We become more able to say no to those we love. Owning the expressing our fear of abandonment teaches us that we can experience the fears and still survive. We gradually learn that our fear of abandonment as adults has simply been carried over from our childhood. The fear we feel now is the same fear we felt at three years of age. While the fear was warranted then, now it is nothing more than an unnecessary and destructive relic of the past. Finally, feeling our grief helps us to heal many of those old, emotional wounds from our childhood. Perhaps, through the grace of our Creator, our tears were given to us to wash away so many of those hurts and fears so hard to describe or even remember.

The over-pleasing Nice Guy syndrome is a deeply conditioned way of thinking, feeling and behaving that is tied to our sense of security and even our very survival. Because of this, the process must be slow and gradual, as our personalities shift toward honesty and integrity. This long — and often painful — process can lead us toward wholeness and healthy, intimate relationships with ourselves and others. As we do the work, we will learn to please others because it pleases us. Remember, some of the greatest, most gratifying rewards we will ever receive can come from the caring behaviors we do for others. Those rewards will be the sublime feelings of connection and intimacy that well up inside of us. Those feelings only come, however, when we are strong enough to give and please out of choice, and not out of fear or need.

Confessions of a
Recovering Feminist
by Carolyn Baker

For more than 30 years, I have defined myself as a feminist. As a feminist, I not only struggled ardently for three decades on behalf of women's equality in every aspect of human existence, but more specifically, I believed that female values were more desirable than male values, and that patriarchy (a way of living based on power and control) was synonymous with masculinity and male values.

Today I am a person in recovery — recovery from alcoholism and various other addictions. For me, recovery is above all else, a process — a process which is constantly in flux and never completely finished. In fact, I have come to believe that the very nature of life itself is process.

Recently I wandered into a bookstore in another state thinking that I might obtain a copy of *Fire In The Belly: On Being A Man*, by Sam Keen. When I asked the woman proprietor if there was a men's section in the store, she looked bewildered and replied, "Other than the lesbian and women's studies section, we believe that every other part of the store is the men's section, because men run the world." When I asked if there was a section pertaining to men's recovery, she answered, "Well, some people are asking for that Robert Bly book, but that's about it."

With some exceptions, this is essentially the kind of response I hear when I speak with my feminist sisters about the men's mythopoetic movement which finally made the cover of *Newsweek* a few weeks ago. Many women take a dim view of female interest in the men's movement and wonder why women like me aren't putting more, instead of less, energy into the women's movement these days.

My answer to that question is that my own healing process has made painfully clear to me that after a lifetime of struggling for gender equity and determination to be seen and treated as whole human beings, it is now time for the women's movement (feminist or otherwise) to look within at its own shadow. Earlier in the struggle, it was necessary to focus on our victimization as women which has not ended and which we must continually challenge. But in the process of healing from any kind of victimization, it becomes crucial at some point to turn inward and face the dark parts of the soul that are inevitably foisted on the victim in the ordeals of oppression.

I recently watched a talk show in which a famous feminist attorney and feminist psychologist were accompanying a courageous woman who had just won a lawsuit against her father for childhood sexual abuse. The mood of the survivor was one of vitality, wisdom, empowerment and warmth. Meanwhile, the two feminist professionals spouted rhetoric and took snide potshots at patriarchy. At one point, the psychologist stated that more than 90 percent of child sexual assault is committed by males. She went on to imply that basically women just don't do this sort of thing, and children are much safer with women. Having been severely abused by women myself and having worked with survivors of all forms of abuse for over a decade, I was aghast at such ignorance and self-righteousness.

The real truth is that women do physically, sexually, emotionally, intellectually and spiritually abuse other human beings. We have been as ecologically irresponsible as males, insisting on disposable diapers, pre-packaged convenience foods, fur coats and "throw-away" everything. We are as guilty of emotional incest (for example, relating to our children as surrogate spouses) as men are. In *Iron John*, Robert Bly speaks of all the subtle nuances of the mother-son wound. He reminds us that tribal societies knew the devastating consequences of older males' not taking responsibility to mentor younger males, and that women, regardless of how well-intentioned, cannot provide the same things for their sons emotionally as men can. Likewise, Marion Woodman's works are replete with reminders of the wounds that all children incur at the hands of "unmothered mothers."

Although many feminists would shudder in horror at the thought of having an "inner male," any human being who is truly self-reflective will acknowledge the presence of an inner opposite. The male in all of us who can change the oil, master the computer or backpack the wilderness is as wounded as our femaleness has been in a male-dominated culture. In the struggle to reclaim "womanpower" and "womanspace," feminists have failed to own the positive values, as well as the wounding, of the inner male. I agree with Woodman's assertion that when women deny the woundedness of the inner male, we become "possessed" by the negative aspects of the wound and gain our gender equity at the expense of our wholeness, turning into extensions of patriarchy in female bodies.

Projection is a crucial underpinning of the patriarchal principle, i.e., "I'm fine, and if everyone else would just change, we would all be fine."

Many women are making their descent into the psyche and the dark night of the soul that looking at the feminine shadow entails. Similarly, many men are making their descents into the "hairy, scary, wet, swampy places" of Bly's Iron John. What is becoming increasingly apparent to me is how much both women and men need each other's journeys. To become whole individuals and whole as a planet, we must value, and hopefully dialog about our personal confrontations with inner demons. Much of the men's movement is about men's acknowledging the wounding of their inner feminine and healing the wound through deep grief, connection with nature, the senses, the body, and finding nurturing and support from each other. Men journeying on this path have learned much from the women's movement and finally see their own wounds in ours. If women are willing to look at their shadow, they will ultimately find somewhere in the psyche a wounded male, and if we are open, there is much the men's movement can show us about the healing of that part of ourselves.

In my opinion, political feminism and the "blame game," as Sam Keen calls it, is outdated. It may be that the last stage of the women's movement (a long, hard look at our inner demons) will be what is clearly the first stage of the men's movement. Nevertheless, we can no longer afford to ignore each other's journeys. The bigger picture is about world peace and balanced ecosystems. Ultimately, these depend on women and men honoring and talking with each other with respect to how we have all been wounded by the war, work and gender-role ethic of the Western, technological mind. I agree with Keen's challenge that "What the majority of men have not done is confront the feminist analysis and world view and sort out the healing treasures from the toxic trash." The women's movement is not dead, but stagnant and stalled — not so much because of Reagan or Bush or an evil external "patriarchy," but because we are not yet willing to take responsibility for the female shadow and the inner patriarchy. The price we pay for refusing to do so is much too great, for as Keen writes: "We are all huddled together on a worldwide battlefield, brothers and sisters in a nuclear family, one race, indivisible, with destruction and fallout for all."

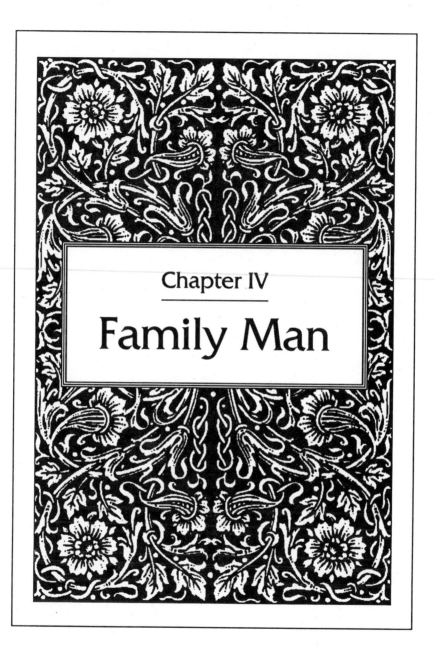

Chapter IV

Family Man

Full Circle

by Jonathan Holden

(for Alan Nordby Holden, 1904-1985)

Scared, I watch my son, eleven, his first
time on the mound, stare in
at the tiny lead-off man.
So tense he's poker-faced,
Zack's practicing the politician's trick
of looking confident, as if a man
could be substantial just by looking it.
But pitching, I learned young, isn't politics.
In the center of that dusty ring
where, as if under some unremitting examination
by the lights, your squirmy shadow's multiplied
by five, faking doesn't work.
The one thing not to do, I told him earlier,
is issue walks. We were playing catch.
I whipped one back. I was talking
as casually as I could, worried
about tonight, but trying to hide it,
to talk seductively, I was talking
in teasy little parables, embroidering them —
about the time I walked eight batters in a row,
about the time I got mad at the umpire
and started to cry — anything to make sure
what help I gave the boy would register
before he'd be alone there on the mound,
out of range. His low fastball stung
my hand. I whipped it back. I told him
how sometimes in the middle of a game
if you get wild you can think about
your stride or where your shoulders face,

you can experiment, correct yourself.
As I talked and threw and talked, we never broke
the easy to-and-fro of pitch and catch,
the more I talked the better
I remembered how. I understood
my own shock when my father used to pause
from his obsessive work to talk to me, to offer —
always shrewdly, at a slight oblique —
what help he could. Zack throws.
The batter takes. Ball one. Ball two. Ball three.
And I prepare myself for the first of many walks.
Zack pauses, on the next pitch eases up.
It's nicked foul. Impassive, Zack waits
for the ball. He delivers easy,
call strike two. If the advice is right
and handed out with style
we never forget the things our fathers say.
They talk directly to our sons,
and our sons can deliver us
our own boyhood back a second time.
The batter whiffs. We live redundantly,
and the second time is better than the first.

Unwed Father

by Thom R. McFarland

When Mary Ellen kept the baby, where did that leave me, the unwed father? I was not a teenager; I was 32, moderately middle class, and hardly ready for unplanned paternity.

New Year's Eve, 1979, Mary Ellen and I slept together, a pleasant enough experience of casual, recreational sex that so many of us indulged in back then. In the heat of passion, I asked about birth control and she huskily replied, "Don't worry. Everything's OK." She didn't bother with the diaphragm because she was sure she wasn't ovulating.

The next few weeks of the new decade, she slept with two other men, also without using the diaphragm. She later admitted to me that she got pregnant "accidentally on purpose."

Two months later, I heard through the grapevine of our East Texas college town that Mary Ellen was pregnant. I started counting on my fingers and got very nervous. While visiting another friend, I encountered Mary Ellen, and confronted her about the pregnancy. She smiled and sighed happily, "I've been meaning to talk to you about that," she said. "You're one of the potential fathers, but don't worry. I'm doing just fine."

"What about me!" I exploded. "What about my feelings!"

I felt angry, used, frustrated, and powerless. I couldn't afford a child financially or emotionally. I was leaving for L.A. to teach and to get an MFA degree. I asked Mary Ellen to please stay in touch and let's try to come to some sort of decision before I left in August and before she had the baby. She never called and neither did I.

That spring, I felt despondent and confused. I considered calling her about an abortion, although I had heard through the infamous grapevine that Mary Ellen considered the baby hers and hers alone, and that nothing would stop her from having this child.

While contemplating abortion, I saw two young boys splashing in the swimming pool where I did laps. Then it hit me. If their parents had chosen abortion, they wouldn't be there. I couldn't ask that of Mary Ellen and her baby. Right then, I accepted the birth of the child.

I left for L.A. in August, 1980. Shawn Gerald Griffen was born September 8, 1980. A blue-eyed boy. The potential black father was out of the running, leaving only me, a blue-eyed blond like Shawn, and Milton, a brown-haired, brown-eyed young man who had slept with Mary Ellen seven months before. I still didn't know who was the father, but the evidence certainly pointed toward me.

Mary Ellen never wrote or called and I too maintained silence. I met Shawn a year later on my visit to East Texas and even held him in my arms, but felt nothing. Could this squirming baby be my son?

I tried venting with friends, but they got tired of listening. "So what if it's your kid," they said. "She chose to have it — not you. Blow it off."

I couldn't. WASP guilt and sense of responsibility wore heavily. I sought counseling at the university health center and explained the problem: I needed to explore my feelings and decide what to do. At the first session, the counselor, a post-doctoral student doing an internship in clinical psychology, suggested the obvious. Call her. I did, told her of my guilt, and wanted to look into paternity tests. Mary Ellen was friendly and supportive, not at all the reception I expected.

I discovered that the paternity tests available at the time, Spring 1982, were a combination of blood and skin samples. These were only 95-percent valid, and required the mother, child, and all potential fathers to participate. The tests cost $125 per person — steep for me at the time.

Since the looks and the timing indicated me, I made the decision. I would be Shawn's daddy and contribute a modicum of child support.

For Shawn's second birthday, September, 1982, I sent a birthday card and as I signed it, "Love, Daddy," I cried. I had become a father.

Although I had spent little time with my son, Mary Ellen and I exchanged numerous letters, even after I left for Saudi Arabia in Fall, 1983. About a week before I returned to Texas the next spring, I got my first Father's Day card. A smiling Charlie Brown addressed the audience, "You've done a marvelous job of being a dad..." and continued on the inside, "...especially considering I didn't come with any instructions!" A perfect card, since Shawn had picked it out. On the back of the card, Shawn had scribbled my name at the top, his in the middle, and his mother's at the bottom.

That summer, 1984, immediately after I had returned, I discovered that Mary Ellen had fallen out of her loft and was paralyzed from the waist down. I searched for her for two months. Finally, through the infamous grapevine again, I located her in a Houston hospital.

I called and made arrangements to spend a weekend with Mary Ellen, Shawn, and Mary Ellen's mother.

Although understandably nervous about all three at once, the weekend was perfect. The two women put me at ease and I couldn't get over what a charmer my son had become. Even the waitress at the Mexican restaurant we visited remarked, "¡Que bonito!"

After my sojourn to Saudi Arabia, I returned to Austin and Mary Ellen and Shawn moved to nearby Wimberly, where I could visit my son every weekend. We actually have formed a relationship like that of any divorced father and son. Mary Ellen has since married a good man who has been supportive in my efforts to build a relationship with Shawn. Shawn's even called me "Daddy" a few times, although he usually calls me Thom.

One recent incident in East Texas summed up my experience as an unwed father. Shawn and I were strolling through Pecan Park, hand-in-hand, during one of those perfect days the gods sometimes grant Texas in August. Shawn looked up at me and drawled in the quaint, East Texas accent he has acquired, "Thom, I just luv evverybody!"

Sometimes, on my good days, I feel the same way.

The Myth of the Dangerous Dad
by Jed Diamond

As a psychotherapist specializing in family relationships, I have been pleased to see the issue of child sexual abuse getting public attention. When I thought of my own children, I couldn't remain professionally detached. I felt a blind rage when I read about people who were accused of abusing small children.

However, I was stunned when once I was accused of "touching the girls inappropriately" at my 10-year-old daughter's elementary school where I volunteered as a teacher's helper once a week.

What for me was an innocent gesture, putting my arm around a shoulder as I knelt to help a student, was seen as suspect by the classroom teacher. I wanted to run away and hide. I knew I hadn't done anything improper, yet I felt soiled. I said nothing.

Weeks later, I finally was able to bring up the incident in my men's group. There were eight of us who had been meeting weekly for six years to discuss our feelings and become closer friends. Was I the only one who had been touched by the fear, I asked. I found that most of the men had their own horror stories to tell. A number of men had friends who had actually had their children taken away on the basis of someone's accusation of child molestation. "I'm afraid to even touch my friends' children, anymore," Dick, a 42-year-old father of three children from Berkeley, said with real sadness. "I used to wrestle with them and throw them up in the air. I played with them like I would my own daughter. Now, I worry that I'll be thought of as a 'dirty old man,' or even worse."

"My daughter, Laurie, just turned nine," said Les, a 45-year-old father from San Francisco, married for the second time. "Lately, when I give her a pat on the bottom, like I've always done, I get a look from my wife which says I've done something wrong. I don't get it."

I had joined the men's group, like the other men, to learn to be more feeling, especially with my wife and children. Now that we were taking the first tentative steps to be more open, we felt the doors being closed in our faces. It didn't seem fair.

During the '80s, this unwarranted fear of men became so widespread that *Nurturing News*, the longest continually published national quarterly addressing the nurturing characteristics of men and boys, devoted a special issue to child molestation (March, 1985).

While deploring child sexual abuse, the journal also warned about the negative backlash against men. According to David Giveans, editor, "Child molestation is not a male only club. Children need nurturing touch from both males and females that is intimate without being sexual."

Only one percent of child-care workers were male at the time the magazine covered this problem. Many experts are concerned that this tiny number may soon become zero if the fear of men is not checked. Almost all believe this would be a tragedy for men, women, and especially for the children.

Sandy Ruben, president of the Boston Association for the Education of Young Children, and Lee Block, an early childhood educator, spoke to the frustration many men feel in an article entitled, "Male Child Care Workers Speak Out on Child Sexual Abuse." "When we were hired, we were asked questions like, 'Could we change diapers?' 'Could we comfort a child whose parent just ran out the door late for work?' But now the undercurrent seems to be, 'Should we even be allowed to work in child care at all?' "

How is it, I thought, that we find it so easy to assume men are "dangerous?" Dr. Warren Farrell, clinical psychologist and author of the internationally acclaimed book, *Why Men Are the Way They Are*, suggests it is a result of what he calls the "New Sexism." He writes, "In the past quarter century, we exposed biases against other races and called it racism, and we exposed biases against women and called it sexism. Biases against men we call humor." He cites numerous examples of "funny" cartoons and stories in various women's magazines which portray men as dogs, wolves, turkeys, sharks, worms and guppies.

Objectification of a group is a prerequisite for rejecting, hurting, or even killing them. Objectification of women is a prerequisite for the rapist. Objectification of Vietnamese as "gooks" was a prerequisite for dropping bombs on them.

We have not yet raised our awareness to see that objectifying men as "potential child-molesters" leads to depriving men of their place in the family and their connection with their children.

John, a 38-year-old Bay Area businessman, has gone through hell in the last three years. He was given custody of his two children after a lengthy divorce and custody battle. His wife, June, had mistreated the children on a number of occasions when she had been drinking, but was allowed visitation rights. On one of the visits, she failed to return the children. "I went out of my mind with worry," John said, with tears in his eyes. John's voice began to rise with anger as he continues. "When I finally found them, she accused me of molesting my 3-year-old daughter. I spent two years and $25,000 proving the accusations were false. I was completely cleared of all child-molestation charges, but the stigma of being accused carried into the civil case and in the end, I lost custody and now see the children only once a month."

Unfortunately, John's experience is becoming increasingly common. In the highly charged atmosphere now surrounding child abuse, being male and being accused is often all that is needed for people to assume one is guilty.

A San Francisco attorney, Fred Butler, understands what divorced men feel when they seek to maintain contact with their children. Butler, 44, who specializes in family law, went through a difficult court battle to get shared custody of his 2-year-old daughter. He now volunteers for Equal Rights for Fathers, an organization concerned with the rights of children, parents and second families. "I believe in shared custody," says Butler. "Children need the opportunity to have continued care from both parents."

Traditionally, both men and women believed that parenting was really mother's job. When Mom and Dad separated, it was assumed that children would be better off staying with her.

"All that has changed," Butler says. "As more and more women are getting involved in the work world, men are more deeply involved with their children. Men are now beginning to fight for their rights to continue to be fathers, even after divorce."

Jerry Johnson, host of KCBS radio's weekly program, "Man to Man," raised the question of whether more men were being falsely accused of molestation. His guest, David L. Corwin, M.D., president of California Professionals on the Abuse of Children, had some startling things to say. "There is an increased awareness of child sexual abuse," said Corwin. "But along with it, there is an increase in the number of men being falsely accused. And this can be absolutely devastating for a man."

Of course, we must protect children from "inappropriate touching" by men or women. However, experts in the area of sexuality are worried that in our zeal to protect children from abuse, we may be creating future dysfunction. According to Margretta Dwyer, University of Minnesota sex therapist, "Touch-deprived children will become the next generation's sexually dysfunctional adults."

Dwyer encourages fathers, teachers and other caretakers to continue to touch children in normal ways. "Because caretakers fear being accused of sex abuse," observes Dwyer, "many children grow up touch-deprived."

Until we change our attitudes, men's fear of touching will continue to increase. All men are vulnerable. Some men are even afraid to change diapers or bathe their children for fear of being accused. Are men being paranoid? Dr. Farrell thinks not.

Farrell notes that by 1986, department stores like J.C. Penney routinely allowed mothers into their sons' dressing rooms, but not fathers into even a 5-year-old daughter's dressing room. When sued for discrimination, Penney responded, "The public perception is that men are voyeurs and molesters." Farrell says, "In the past decade, liberation has meant fathers going from 'Daddy knows best' to 'daddies molest.' "

What are men to do? One of the men in my group said it this way: "It's time that we broke our silence about ways in which we are labelled as 'jerks.' It's time we stopped accepting and laughing at jokes that classify men as less than human. It's time we spoke out in the classroom and with our friends and family. It's time we gathered support from men and women who are opposed to sexism directed at men, not just that directed at women. It's time we loved and touched our children without fear."

It's time we put to rest, forever, the "myth of the dangerous dad."

Tales of Uncle Nap
by James McGrath

The Suspenders and Belly of Uncle Nap

Millie said, "It's a funny thing, but when you get old and remember those you loved, you only remember the good, never the bad, which proves the bad didn't count anyway. . .

"Now, your Uncle Nap's belly, you remember how his big suspenders sort of held him together and how he would rub both his hands across that world of a thousand and a thousand good meals from your Aunt Sinnie and he would lean against the old maple or the pillar on the porch and pull the suspenders aside as if his belly was taking a deep breath."

Yes. Uncle Nap had a glorious belly. I could never reach around him when we hugged. I loved it when I could put my head against his belly. There were sounds like the river cataracts over by the covered bridge. There was a warmth from all the baked bread and honey we ate together on autumn nights when the maple turned gold. And his plaid shirts were always tightly rolled around his belly — never a broken button. And his belly looked so hard and firm, but my face could get lost in its softness like in the feather pillow upstairs in the cold. Uncle Nap smelled so good. There were the brown dribbles of his Copenhagen just above mid-line. It was pungent and once I got a taste of its hot sourness. There was the smell of the early morning fires around his belly — I liked that smell best. The suspenders left long faded streaks along his belly — from his rounded shoulders to the edge of his blue overalls.

Once I was sure that Uncle Nap was Santa Claus because his belly jiggled when he laughed. I never saw jelly jiggle, but I saw Uncle Nap's belly jiggle and that made me smile and think about him every time I heard the Christmas story. I've never seen such a perfect belly as Uncle Nap's. Aunt Effie said he got it from drinking beer. I really didn't believe her because I only saw him drink beer once and his belly never got any bigger.

Uncle Nap and His Big Black Shoes

When Uncle Nap was young, he did not wear shoes. His feet had toughened all spring and summer and fall so that during the winter he could run about, do his chores and fill his days and nights barefooted. Besides that, young Chehalis Indian men were strong enough and did not need shoes; it was the white settlers who needed shoes, he used to say.

As he grew older and became more involved around the fort near Chehalis in the early 1900s, and the trappers and the work became more involved with inside things as well as outside things, his mentor gave him a pair of big work shoes. He looked sort of strange — the only Indian man with big, black, heavy leather shoes.

He wore them about the Fort tending the horses — actually he found them helpful when the horses got rambunctious. But when he left the Fort every day for the village, he always took the shoes off; at first he waited until he got to the edge of the woods. Later, he wore them through the woods to the clearing where the big stumps were and the huckleberries. Then, after several months, he would wear them through the woods, across the clearing until the middle fork of the Newaukum River. Then he'd take off those black shoes, carry them across the river and on into the brush near the village, where he hid them.

He did not want the old people to see those big, black shoes. About this time, his aunt gave him a pair of elk skin moccasins — winter was going to be bad this year, she said. He was so happy. He gave her his first deer to skin that winter.

Uncle Nap wore those elk skin moccasins all winter. The men at the fort at first asked where his black shoes were. He said, "I have them at home being sealed in duck fat." All winter, he wore his moccasins about the fort and his black shoes were in the bushes by the village. He would visit those shoes at least once a week to try them on. And, yes, he did rub duck fat into them to give them a softness like the spring coming up after the hard winter.

Collecting Agates

I walked across the covered wooden bridge over the Newaukum River. It was the bridge that rumbled at night when the old cars crossed the loose planks. I wanted to walk through the bridge, stop in the middle, lie down on a broken plank and spit down through the spider webs into the river, through the dark places. Then I'd walk on into the sundust of the dirt road, up the hill past the Aunt's place where the hogs always wandered around, and the dump was glittering with Carnation milk cans and blue milk of magnesia bottles.

There were acres of giant rotting fir tree stumps up the road where honeysuckle vines climbed about and brake ferns unrolled their green webbed spirals. Further on, after the big patch of pink fireweed, there was a great, wild blackberry patch where I could stain my fingers and spend the next mile before the road turns licking the purple stains until only the finger tips blushed near the nails.

I found the cow path off to the right after the road bend that led me to the river itself. Uncle Nap first brought me here to show me where the best agates were. And I always started out on the same sandbar splotched with fresh cow pies that buzzed with those stinging yellow flies. All about the sandbar were scattered bits of jasper, some petrified wood, quartz and those wondrous flat stones that would skip and hop across the pools in the river when they were thrown just right. When I could skip one seven times, I would stop.

From the first big sandbar, I would wander upstream. I knew where the trout hid, and where a river otter lived. I knew where the water ouzel bounced near a rapid and where I could always find a pair of burrowing owls. But I really had come to find agates. And now as I look back, the best agates were always in Uncle Nap's eyes when I came back home across the covered bridge.

Dust Devils

It was 40 years ago that Uncle Nap and I last held one another. I was on my way to teach in Germany. He was standing by the grey plank gate. Aunt Sinnie was under the maple tree twisting her faded, flowered apron. The night before we had sat on the old Ford rumble seat on the porch watching the car lights on Highway 99. "There won't be any rain tomorrow. The Big Dipper is straight up, holding all the water in."

Tonight under the new moon I can look around me on my La Cieneguilla land and know that I learned to share my life with the seasons. I know the cycles of the locust trees, the cottonwoods, the willows, and the voices of the blue heron, the magpie, the red fox; the tracks of a buck and a doe, the smell of spring oozing in the tree saps by the river, and brittle stems of gramma grass dancing. I found where the bull snakes shed their skins and the bluebirds feed.

There may not be any trout in the pools of the Santa Fe River, but in the Newaukum River heart that I carry with me each day, Uncle Nap smiles with a bit of brown Copenhagen juice at the corner of his mouth and whispers:

"Have a safe journey."

"Keep your eyes on the ground."

"Hurry home."

I never knew when Uncle Nap actually died. I feel the softness of his shadow about me on hot summer days, and his sweet warmth in winter when I walk about my land. The sparkle of dew on the zucchini in late spring is from his eyes, and his laughter tumbles down my road in dust devils. I stand at the corner post of my grey plank gate and swing it open for the dust devils to pass through on their way toward home, dissolving into the black basalt wall of petroglyphs above the house. My grandson Dustin will be coming soon. He'll be 7 this June.

Uncle Nap

Uncle Nap passed through the world like a ghost
searching for memories,
waiting for me to come to him
so he could tell me the stories

that were of our blood.
Stories for the men of the world;
stories for warriors and poets,
and hunters of dreams.

The stories that Uncle Nap told me were about
tree places where bees swarmed and made sweet love;
river places where we could crawl out on logs
to watch trout;

meadow places where huckleberries grew
on burnt-out cedar stumps;
plowed fields where his family village once stood
and only bits of arrowheads and sod mounds remained.

In my child's eye as the nephew to my Indian Uncle,
I learned that the trees and river and huckleberries
and secrets and land held are for us
to make dreams from, and poems and shadows.

New Rites for Fathers and Daughters

By Gordon Clay

A recurring theme in all the retreats I have attended and presented in the past 16 years is the impact of the father on his children. Whether present, abusive, distant, perfect, or absent, the father's effect is profound. For sons, the father often determines how the child will see himself as a man and how he will respond to women. For a daughter, the father influences how she will see men, how she will be treated by men and how she will act around them.

Having been a parent since 1965, I have come to believe that no matter what we do as fathers, we will still occasionally mess up. Yet I firmly believe that by becoming more aware and doing more work on our relationships with our children throughout their lives, especially during the tumultuous years of adolescence, we can have a very positive impact on them that will effect at least seven generations to come. While improved communication is important, we actually need to develop completely new models for positive ways fathers can be with our children, and especially our teen-age daughters.

Rituals to Support Cultural Change

There has been a trend during the last 10 years to go back to our more primitive roots and emulate many rites-of-passage that were practiced for thousands of years. We've seen men go into the woods to develop and perform their own rites-of-passage, while others take their sons in an attempt to bring back some of that tradition that has been missing the last few hundred years (except through initiations like a bar mitzvah or confirmation, the first drink at home, the first car, the first sexual experience or the military).

When we look at these recent developments in our culture, however, there seem to be two important elements missing. The first involves the setting of sacred space, whether a rite-of-passage for a teen or adult male. I believe that we must set this space with the intention of opening it up, at some point, and invite women to experience and participate in our celebration and acknowledgment, and do some of the follow-up work in context with women. Not only does this bring great exhilaration to see women enter this space, it gives us a place to check things out, to see how we react, and to see how women react — not with the intention of changing things to please women, but to see how our progress is being experienced. This offers an opportunity for important feedback that may provide welcome insight. And, it breaks down the system of separation that our ancient ancestors felt was appropriate in their culture. There are too many current examples using reverse discrimination to counteract discrimination. How confusing this picture must seem to our children! This system of exclusion no longer serves our changing and growing cultural system, which is based on the inclusion of all people, regardless of sex, age, race, religion, looks, etc. We, as men, can and must take on the responsibility of removing this confusion from our personal, parental and public work. By periodically opening our sacred space, to invite women in, we will be able to teach our children by example that separate space is appropriate if it isn't developed to exclude others on a permanent basis.

Secondly, men have historically initiated boys, and women initiated girls into the same-sex-role obligations practiced by their culture at the time. While I think this can and should be done in our current cultural climate, again we, as men, must look at how our culture is changing and develop additional rituals to support these changes.

One of the major shifts, seen for the first time in any culture, is that many of our daughters go into areas of livelihood that have traditionally been the exclusive domain of men. And, while many men have been taking their sons into the wilderness to re-enact some form of ancient male rites-of-passage, this cultural change cries out for new rituals that also acknowledge and support our daughters as they go into the world.

A New Rite-of-Passage

As a single parent for more than 13 years, it was the realization of this need that brought me and my daughter, Natalie (then 21), together to develop and co-lead a new rite-of-passage. What developed was a weekend retreat in the wilderness with a group of fathers and their teen-age daughters.

We began by acknowledging the child in each of our daughters. At the same time, we wanted the fathers to get back in touch with their own child-like qualities of joy, play and silliness. From there, we developed rituals to bring up and confront our daughters' fear of growing up and our fears of seeing them grow up. In this process, it was important to let her do things completely on her own while letting her know that she wasn't alone — that there were others, in addition to her father, whom she could go to for support. We next provided opportunities that required cooperation with the other initiates, while making it clear that each daughter was totally responsible for the actions she chose to take — two important lessons for all to learn! We closed the wilderness retreat with a great ceremony welcoming our daughters into our world. Each man had secretly brought something that had been passed down from his father (her grandfather). As each father passed this gift down another generation, he told about his own father and about the gift.

As we prepared to close our camp, we turned over the leadership responsibility to our daughters. They were to organize and direct the closure of the campgrounds, create a closing ritual and guide the return trip, with the fathers assisting only when asked.

Using these more traditional aspects of rites-of-passage, we were careful to ensure that each process supported the changing cultural perspective and acknowledged each girl's uniqueness and personal power. Thus, we built acknowledgment of her separateness and difference from her mother and let go, at the same time, of our need to protect her. This allowed each girl to explore her own limits to learn that she was capable of doing much more on her own and without our help than she had ever thought possible. The importance of the father acknowledging this in his daughter can't be over-emphasized. Simply looking at how we unknowingly have treated our daughters differently than our sons, often over-protecting and demonstrating rather than letting them risk by exploring and doing things on their own.

Men Still Make the Best Fathers

But where do these skills come from? The fact is that fathers are inherently very good at loving and cuddling their children as well as disciplining and setting boundaries and limits. They can be gentle or roughhouse, go on roller coasters and play house. They enjoy playing with dolls as much as playing ball. The fact is that fathers are full of affection and tenderness as well as strength and power. They are caring, emotional nurturers who are open, sensitive and vulnerable. And, it is this vulnerability that encourages them to show not only their strengths but their weaknesses so that their daughter can learn to accept these aspects of herself and others.

Being a father today, however, contradicts the fundamental ways most men have been raised. And, while the woman's role has expanded into the traditionally male arena, many men who have taken on more responsibility for child rearing have found little acceptance in the workplace, community or among many of their friends. These men suffer from the residual effects of years of cultural thinking that has said child rearing isn't as important as earning money. Add to this the cultural fear of the father-daughter connection. "Why," people question, "would a father want to go into the wilderness, alone, with his daughter?" The answer is the same for a man with a daughter as with a son — to share the wilderness with her, to teach her, to spend special time with her, to show her that the wilderness isn't just for men, but something to be experienced and enjoyed by all.

Yet, the sexual implication and challenge remains, if not on the surface, just below in the looks and thoughts of many.

Sexual Distancing

Fathers have a major impact on their daughters' view of their own femininity and sexuality and some are very good at accepting their display of sexuality in stride. As she goes through puberty, the underlying attraction between them is understood and the father acknowledges these feelings, confirming that he, too, is a sexual being. Unfortunately, as our daughters move through this time and start to develop physically, sexually and emotionally, some fathers withdraw from their daughters. This usually happens because the father isn't clear about how to react, how to work with the feelings that are inside of him, and how to deal with the sexual energy his daughter is displaying.

Since most men don't talk about problems with other men, many fathers who feel this sexual energy, think they are the only ones, that they must be really perverted. Drawing away from a developing daughter at this time, however, can be very damaging to her sexuality and affect how she will act around boys and men in the future. This doesn't mean that she should tolerate inappropriate behavior. It only says that the energy is there, it is normal, and that we must not withdraw our love, affection, hugs and kisses lest we negatively affect not only our relationship with our daughter, but her future relationships with men.

Additionally, this culture has developed such fear around sex that inappropriate taboos have been created that further confuse the situation. When the taboo doesn't fit human experience, a situation can develop that clouds right from wrong and may open up more inappropriate sexual activity than would otherwise be present.

We need to develop healthy messages that separate touch from sex and sex from intimacy. We need to talk with other men about our experiences so that we will know that we aren't the only men feeling this sexual energy. We need to be able to recognize the appropriate limits of parental love and distinguish what is healthy from what we should be concerned about. While somewhat simplistic, if you are comfortable showing affection with others around, it's usually healthy, whether others are around or not. If you feel the need to make it a secret, it's at least borderline, if not totally inappropriate. (The Ehrenbergs' book, *The Intimate Circle: The Sexual Dynamics of Family Life*, provides some valuable information about appropriate and inappropriate sexual intimacy between fathers and daughters and would be a valuable addition to any personal library.)

Making the Commitment

It has become my belief that the importance of a close, healthy father-daughter relationship is possibly the most needed and important relationship a father can develop at this time in our culture. It will provide daughters and women with a positive image of a father, which is currently missing, for all intent and purpose.

This change won't come about merely by taking your teen-age daughter into the wilderness for a rite-of-passage, though it's never too late to start. It should begin by making a commitment to be involved from the start and make the care of your children as important as your work. It means working for a company that supports parental leave, not just in theory but in practice. It means taking a job that has the flexibility so that you can take off when your children need you and that allows, and encourages, ample time to be with them. It means letting the boss and people you work with know that you take fathering seriously and encourage other fathers to do the same. It means placing as much importance on your active involvement with daughters as you do with sons.

It's not about parental rights, it's about parental obligations. It's the only way men will ever know the absolute joy and excitement of fathering. When it comes down to the short strokes, I've never known of a father to say on his death bed, "I wish I'd worked more." So, don't place children second to your work. And, don't place daughters second to your sons. A greeting card I once read said, "A man who has a daughter has the richest treasure." Make the commitment to uncover that treasure. Start working to bring the bright sheen back and cherish it forever!

For Chuck

by Lyman Grant

We've been very sad around our house this summer. In July, my wife's father died. It occurred suddenly. He went into the hospital for tests on a Tuesday, and by Friday he was dead. Yes, we've been sad, and because much of this issue concerns fathers, putting this issue together has not allowed us to hide from our grief by working.

It seems that we all are, in some way, mourning for our fathers, but grieving my father-in-law's death is different. Because Chuck Adams was a generous, adventurous, open, loving man, my wife and I have experienced a large measure of joy in our grief. I knew Chuck for only seven years. Most of the time he lived 200 miles away, so we saw each other only six or seven times a year. Three years ago, he and Winnie, my mother-in-law, moved within 20 miles of us so they could be closer to my wife, their only child, and to our son Will, who is now five years old. From that time on, I had the pleasure of seeing him once a week. He loved driving his truck, so we never knew when he and Winnie might show up.

Imagine. In this society, a thirtysomething couple who enjoys, even looks forward to, seeing her parents every week. But that's the kind of parents my wife has, the kind of man Chuck was. From the day I met him, he made me feel accepted and respected as a man, but in a kindly, low-keyed way. I teach English in a community college, so he liked to tease me and call me "professor." I had the feeling, however, that very little was expected of me "in the real world." All I had to do to keep his respect was to love his daughter and treat her accordingly. A couple of years later, our son joined our family, and by the way he loved that grandson, I knew he had raised his expectations. Now to keep his respect I had to love my wife and my son.

To him, careers were fine, something that one should take seriously — Chuck had risen fairly high in the government bureaucracy as a safety engineer, and when I received a promotion to midlevel administration, he bought me a briefcase — but for Chuck, one's family was where life really took place. He was a happy man, but I never saw him happier than the times he would crawl around on his knees and jump from behind a door to scare his grandson or the time he presented Will with a set of homemade bow and arrows, the arrows tipped with pencil erasers, or the times Will would find that extra piece of candy deep inside a pocket.

One is tempted here to tell stories, as his brothers and his in-laws did around the house before and after the funeral: tales of his eating eight pieces of pie at a country reunion or of gracefully indulging his mother-in-law; tales of nights on the town with his brother or of his love of driving on the open road. I am tempted to discuss the joys of playing golf with him or going to a ball game, or how I asked him last December to read Robert Bly's essay for MAN! on the naive male because I wanted to know if as a 76-year-old man he had known any young men who fit Bly's description. He replied that, yes, he knew one — himself.

But the story I have to tell is that of the last gift he gave me. It fell to me to tell my son that his grandfather, his Pop Pop, had died. My son knew that Pop Pop was in the hospital, that he had had a heart operation, but he thought, as we all did, that his Pop Pop was getting better. I picked my son up from day care. We put our seat belts on; then figuring it was wrong to delay and "wait for the right moment," I said that I had to tell him something. "Pop Pop died today." My son took it straight in, and I saw 20 emotions wave through his body, through his innocent face. The last was a shred of denial, "Did he really die?"

"Yes, son, really, just about an hour ago."

Then he looked at me so intently, examining every part of my face. "Are you crying, Dad?"

"Yes, I am."

"Why?"

"Because I am very sad that Pop Pop died, and I will miss seeing him and talking with him very much."

"Me, too," said Will.

We all miss you, Chuck. You always encouraged Sharon and me in creating this journal. More, you lived the values that we are trying to live by. This one's for you, man!

Dragon's Eye

by Robert German

The eternal dragon's eye
which first deifies
then threatens Time
has swallowed up my father,
pulling him through to the other side.
The ornamental doorway
in between the worlds
has rammed shut. Today,
I am left with questions.

Pop, Dad, Daddy, Gene (never Eugene),
whoever he was,
he was the family helmsman, and this
supremacy in him emerged from
some odd, internal seascape.
Steady with the wind, he stayed
subdued and suspicious of extremes
and so sometimes took the battering
that indifferent seas can give.

But it was no contradiction
to see this enemy of excess
also evenly delighted by the
homespun virtues, sobriety and satiety,
and staying close to home. Love he had,
but how rarely it got into open air.
More frequently it was seen in material
endowment. Helmsman, why so remote?
His own mother's binding,
blinding, scarifying love,
legendary in the family lore,
no doubt holds the key.

Withal, his personal cornucopia was
rich with burgher suspicions and success
as well as class-bound prejudice: blacks
and Jews and the wealthy. So educated
a man, why so blind in spots? A religious
man, organized religion charmed him not.
And those who bilked through the pulpit,
selling hell's fire and similar toxic measures,
earned his strongest ire. Here I still agree.
As for the other things? Who is it who is not
sometimes victimized by his times
and class and physical location? I, in my
social lexicon, having long ago left
racial disdain except as occasional raw fear,
still use wealth and greed synonymously.

Beyond the family, the single name
he leaves behind is now cast in raised letters
on a brass plaque clutching a single, public
building in Bellaire. Small monument
for such as he, and one he never mentioned.
Obviously, he took his service seriously.
It comes to me as need and fear. Could I ever
gain his quiet sense of responsibility?

These are questions
of small importance, now.
So definite a man,
so indefinite a father. Father,
I seek you still in blessings
sought from other, older men.
I did it once again this past week,
and know now it must stop.
I must give it up or else use it
to bless the younger men,
the only service I can easily perform
in this fast-fading world.

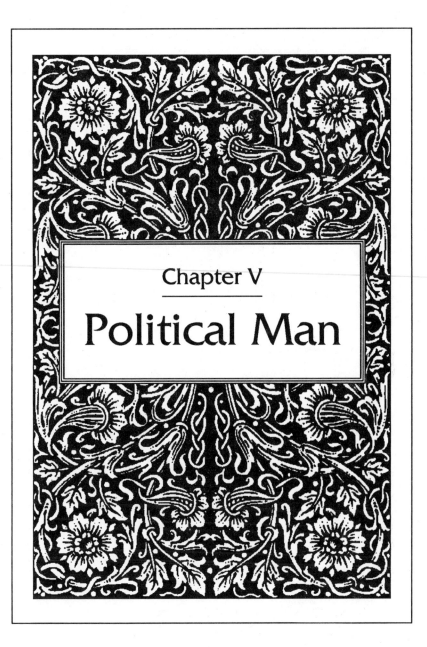

Chapter V

Political Man

What is Male Oppression?
By Rich Armington

A few years before she died, I asked my dad's mom what he was like as a child. She said many things, and near the end added with her shoulders held high, that he never cried. I was about to restate the question, "But what was he like?" when I realized that she actually was telling me something important about what my dad really was like.

Why do you think a cuddly little boy would never cry? No, I mean something else beyond the constant barrage of "big boys don't cry," or "keep crying and I'll give you something to cry about," or "go to your room if you're going to keep that up." Something else. To a cute, innocent three-year-old boy trying to carve a place in his world, crying as a way to rid himself of the effects of multitudes of little and big hurts, makes as much sense as the birds singing softly after a strong rain, or the roar of the falling stream as the mountain snow melt tumbles to the lake below. The world makes so much more sense when we can cry about it.

So I tried another approach with my grandmother, "Why didn't he cry?" Her answer had the ring of something old and dull. I don't even remember what the words were, but I had the sense that there had to be something else to this important question. I think my father was too powerful and bold a little boy to be squashed by only a few adults when he was young. Something else.

At the same time I've come to believe that my dad is a fairly common father. Little I could tell you about him would be shocking to you. That's the idea. My father is like your father, give or take a few years, or states, or children, or pounds. One other thing we have in common is that our dads had it very rough in their world. And it doesn't show only in the inability to cry. It shows in many different ways. In order to understand our dads, we need to understand the larger system they are embedded in — the ways of the world that shape and condition the men that then in turn shape and condition their sons. Then we can more effectively understand ourselves. This conditioning, perpetuated by unexamined myths has a name — it's called Male Oppression.

Male oppression, as a concept which we can work with effectively in our lives, is difficult to lift down from the dusty bookcase of intellectualizing. It's hard to see how to apply it to our lives in a concrete, specific way. But it sure is important—male oppression literally kills men. When left unexplored it certainly bleeds all our relationships of the warmth, joy, passion, creativity, and lightness they deserve. It doesn't destroy them, it just deadens them a bit. Or a lot. Despite how heavy the burdens have been, we have never stopped in our attempts to have mutually challenging, empowering, caring, and supportive relationships. That's what I love about men. Many men are succeeding, and all of us are trying as best we can. There are four things that get in the way:

1. Suppression of Emotional Release: Our natural ability to release our emotions of fear, embarrassment, shame, sadness, or anger through shaking, laughing, crying, or being angry has been systematically curtailed, distorted, unbalanced, and in some instances completely cut off.

2. Military Conditioning: All men (I mean boys) are readied for military service from a very young age. Readied means being conditioned to accept the idea of killing others or being killed ourselves. This occurs regardless of whether or not we go into the military.

3. Over-responsibility: As men we are expected to be so responsible for carrying the burden of the safety and monetary welfare of others, that we actually become overly responsible. This occurs often at the expense of our own safety and welfare.

4. Gay Oppression: We are taught that only homosexual men are affected by gay oppression. This is not true. Every man, regardless of sexual preference, is hit hard with gay oppression. Its major purpose is to create and maintain a rigid, dehumanizing, unattainable model of what it means to be a man. It is also intimately linked with the oppression of females (sexism). And it keeps men effectively isolated and fearful of close, loving

relationships with other men. Gay oppression is not about sex or being gay.

In exploring these four individual pieces of male oppression it may be helpful to think of them as four strands that weave together in a mutually binding manner. As each braid of the oppression is recognized and unwound, the other three elements lose their strength and ability to clamp down so tightly on our lives. How do these four elements: difficulty with release of emotions; military conditioning; over-responsibility; and gay oppression intertwine and relate to each other?

Purpose of Male Oppression

Male oppression is so entrenched and widespread in every structure of our society that it clearly serves a purpose much more profound than simply wanting men to "grow up tough to meet a tough world." What runs the country is a financial system that relies heavily on economic exploitation. This system is primarily overseen by white males. These men have certain "rewards" for being placed into this role. But they have to give up enormous parts of themselves in the process. So much in fact that no man would or does take on this role voluntarily.

The conditioning that forces men into this role occurs covertly and overtly from birth until death; not one of us ever had a chance to say "no thanks; I'll pass." Many times we barely notice the occurrence of male oppression but instead assume "that's the way it is," or "that's the way men are." No one consulted us. It was required that we take on this grinding position.

Suppression of Emotional Release

The "rewards" some men have gained include the opportunity to situate ourselves on top of a heap of entitlement (economic, educational, social, employment, etc.) Everyone belongs on top of the same heap. But this society erroneously believes that exploitation is crucial to continued functioning of the system. So men are readied for the military, in part to protect the heap. Of course the training begins much earlier than boot camp. In fact, it starts at birth. Not paying positive attention to boys' feelings at home or school or in sports or in malls causes these little lovable humans to eventually stop paying attention to their own emotions. The consequences are profound and go far beyond just a difficulty in being able to cry about the more painful parts of our lives. How are these two seemingly disparate pieces bound together — our emotions and the military?

Military Conditioning

A friend told me of his experience in boot camp. One night they were taken out to a dark, flat field and split into two groups. Half of his buddies were given rifles and placed in one group; he was put in the other. He was told to crawl one hundred yards on the ground while his friends in the other group fired tracer bullets (you can see them spinning by in the dark) two feet above his head. He told me that he was absolutely terrified, but knew if he let himself actually feel the terror, he might panic and stand up. Of course that would mean sure and instant death. With "unemotional coldness" he crawled safely to the opposite end. I thought to myself that those early foreboding messages he had surely received as a young boy had ironically saved his life on that dark, flat field. Not much had changed. The refrain, "big boys don't cry" had just become more grown up. As was stated earlier, male oppression is no small matter — it kills. Our conditioning starts early and with a very specific outcome.

Men are set up in the most terrifying situations, even if there is no boot camp in our history. Yet we are not allowed to be scared. Fights in the school yard, or worse, after school with no adults to intervene; contact sports that pit boy against boy; the jobs of miners, construction workers, asbestos workers, taxi drivers, plutonium workers, and police workers all have at least one thing in common — fear. Fear that can only be shown at the risk of more fear, or danger, or humiliation (which can feel like death without support systems to talk about it, release it, and work it through). This engenders tremendous distrust and competition among men. Interactions between men have a fearful, staccato-like quality that makes it difficult for us to slow down and notice the natural humanness in each other. And then we wonder why we act so weird at times!

Over-responsibility

Men seem so willing to take on these dangerous roles and occupations for the same reason many men work two jobs, or long hours, or weekends. We have been conditioned to a life of over-responsibility that keeps us from experiencing closer, more intimate relationships with our families and friends. At the surface this seems so easily changed — "just stop!" But sometimes we don't even know how to create or maintain these types of relationships. And we have been conditioned in repeated and hidden ways to find much of our self-worth in our work. There is so little societal support to alter this chronic tendency towards over-work that it is very confusing and extremely difficult to know how to make the needed changes. Redefining your self-worth and changing society's expectations can seem a bit overwhelming when you're stuck in traffic on the way home after a long day at work.

Gay Oppression

The one thing that goes to the heart of wedging men apart is gay oppression. Gay oppression affects every male. It is not about being homosexual. That is the excuse which is used. This doesn't mean that society does not terrorize homosexual men about their sexuality. Most clearly, it does. Just ask any gay man who has been brave enough to "come out," and you can hear story after story of blistering, intimidating treatment. But the real reason for being brutally mistreated is due to being "different" than the majority. It all starts early: wearing glasses ("Queer!"); walking differently ("Fag!"); holding your books in the wrong manner in school ("Fairy!"); putting your arm around another boy ("Homo!").

At a very early age, boys and girls are separated from each other at play and in school. Lacking equally strong messages and modeling from society, the inaccurate communication to boys is that "it is best to be male in this society." Therefore, the worst to be is "non-male." There are two types of "non-males." The first is female. Boys are taught that girls are "yukky," "sissies." Over the course of many years, and numerous societal statements about females, these susceptible boys then proceed to systematically put girls down in their behaviors and thoughts. This is the beginning of sexism. And importantly, it is also the first stage of gay oppression.

The other type of "non-male" is any male that shows qualities that don't fit into the traditional male role. Boys are taught to discount and cut off parts of themselves that are seen as feminine ("the opposite sex"). Behaviors such as showing hurt, caring, tenderness, crying, or associating with girls, are extremely risky because of the fear of being labeled "sissy" by other boys. This label is more potent than mere name calling — "sissies" are shunned, beaten up, shamed and ridiculed. In later years, any male that steps outside the rigid job description of being male runs the grave risk of being ridiculed and threatened with "fag," "fairy," "gay," "queer." Again, this is no small matter — gay men continue to be pulled from their homes and cars and killed or beaten because they are "different." The purpose of this hurtful conditioning is to make all boys conform, through the threat of gay oppression. The message is frighteningly clear; either you put others down (become an oppressor) or you will be put down (be oppressed).

In this way gay oppression affects all men. If you want to stay close to a man you run the risk of being seen as gay. It is only OK to be heterosexual. And unfortunately, part of what that means is being distant from other men, unfeeling, competitive, aggressive and cerebral. It's a completely inaccurate picture of what men really are like. And to men's enormous credit, courage, and persistence, many have not bought deeply into this conditioning. But it still is embedded deeply in our society.

Overcoming our Oppression

What would a "real" man look like who had escaped this conditioning or had pushed enough rubble off himself to breathe fresh air and walk unencumbered? I think it's what we all seek. To see our true nature means to be completely proud of being a man — strong, creative, loving, cooperative, lighthearted, full of zest and intelligence. The kind of intelligence that seeks out close relationships with men, women and children equally. Intelligence that thinks clearly about how minority groups, women, children, as well as other men have been exploited and hurt. This will enable him to be a much better supporter of each group. Seem unlikely? Well we clearly have the information and resources that no other generation of men have ever had. It certainly can't hurt to get this rubble off our backs. So how do we go about doing it?

The image I have is that every man (men of the working class, middle class, owning class, men of color, differently-abled men, white men, homosexual, bisexual and heterosexual men) would find some place or time in his life in which he feels his true essence — his grounded power, love, and creativity. A place where there is no distinction or conflict between what he wants and what any other man, woman, or child wants. That moment when he can nod inwardly and sigh — "Oh, I understand." I think we have all had at least a moment of that space in our lives at one time or another. Maybe with our family, or alone in the woods, or sitting in traffic staring at a billboard, or at a party, or walking down the hallway of our workplace, or in the bowling alley wearing ill-fitting rental shoes. Somewhere, sometime. And then see that moment as the core truth of who we really are — powerful, loving, creative. Now find ways that allow you to share it with others — the children, men, and women you know, as well as with as many of the men listed previously that you can manage. In the final analysis this is how I think we can shake off the rubble. It's not impossible — it is a hope, but it can also be a reality. Untold treasures are available when we follow our core truth.

More singularly, the way to fight male oppression is to get close to other men. It's that simple. Or difficult. The cornerstone of our conditioning has been isolation. It keeps the oppression quiet, hidden, and in place. Work to create male relationships where you can be vulnerable — talk about what really fuels your love, fear, insecurity, excitement, anger, and humor. All those conversations you generally reserve for home or alone while in your car. Ask another man about his life and then listen closely. And when the relationship becomes difficult (all the close ones do at various times) don't walk away. Seek help to understand what rubble may still lie on top of your best thinking. See it as a time to free yourself more.

In addition, reach out and talk to that man on the bus, or next door, or on the street, or in the gym that you've ignored for years. Find out what's important to him. Reach out to other men — not to save them or "help" them — but because it makes complete sense for you to challenge the bonds that keep you distant from men. This really is for you. Not another thing to do for someone else — we know that path only too well. Just by getting close to other men, we will be breaking the back of each and every element of male oppression.

As I now look back to my conversation with my grandmother, I am quite relieved that I didn't chastise her for what she said about my dad not crying. Because even considering the wonderful things she was able to give him, the issue of my father's life is much larger than his mother — or his father — or his wife — or even him. Realizing this, the question, "who's to blame?" then becomes, "what's the best way out?" Well, my father never had the resources or information to steer very far from the first question. Finding answers to the second question seems more sustaining and empowering to me. What gets passed down to us as children is a much broader issue than just looking to the last link in the chain before ourselves. Blaming the tree limb above us for dropping chilling snow down our backs doesn't help very much, either. It blinds us to creative solutions — like avoiding the tree limb; or running like hell from under it; or asking for help — to shake it off in a warm, safe place with someone who will let us shake.

This Must Be the Place:
An Annotated, Nonlinear, Meditative History of the Men's Movement, Complete with Buckets

by Ric Williams

A funny thing happened on the way to the past — I ran smack dab into the future. Obviously, that's the place to be, but when I started on my journey I wondered how far back I should go. My first thought was to start with Adam. After all, his was the first case in which a man transferred his responsibility for his actions to a woman. And it was our first encounter with the failure to liberate ourselves from the past. These primal ideals of liberation and responsibility are therefore the obvious foundations for a history/overview of the men's movement. But they also must be the two pillars of its future that will remain, no matter how else one defines the men's movement, or it is destined to experience the premature death of Andy Warhol's 15 minutes.

This dichotomy should come as no surprise, as all historical movements of liberation began with the stated or unstated goal of achieving responsibility for one's self and one's actions. The men's movement benefits, however, from all the former liberation movements, because men can identify their basic nature and cast away the chaff while keeping the wheat. The twist for men is this: most liberation movements begin wanting what the master has — freedom from bondage, the right to vote, the right to work, the right to travel, the right to marry whomever one wants, the right to live where one chooses, the right to choose how life will be lived. This struggle in its inchoate form takes on the magical formula of sympathetic magic — like attracts like. So the oppressed mimic the oppressor. Spartacus acted like the Roman patrons. African-Americans straightened their hair and lightened their skin. Women wore no bras, put on pants and found so-called real jobs in the office and factory, as opposed to the denigrated role of mother and housekeeper. Homosexuals voted Republican and loudly proclaimed their normalcy.

In short, liberation begins by denying the individual's uniqueness in society. Victimization and weakness is denied, is pushed into the furthest corner of shadowhood. This denial of the victim and weakness and its resultant horror show in our homes and on our streets is one of the most important aspects of human behavior that the men's movement can hope to illuminate and ultimately transform. It is also its greatest obstacle and, naturally, was an early, and still present pitfall.

So the twist is who does the man imitate in this quest for liberation? Whom does he hope to be like when he comes to the end of the dream? Where is the sympathetic touchstone he must responsibly defend?

The Civil Rights and Gay Rights movements are likely choices and have contributed much, though not as much as they will, for they must be included and not just alluded to if the movement is to succeed in its nurturing goals. But it is feminism that is the obvious place to start. After all, feminists pointed out the classic flaws in the male-dominated culture, the hegemonic patriarchy. They had the idea of encounter groups and other psychological empowerment tools that are used in the men's movement. It was the feminists that Warren Farrell responded to in his 1974 book, *The Liberated Man*, and subsequent interview in *Ms.* that is usually cited as the seminal event of the modern day men's movement. It is that movement he continues to respond to in his current anti-feminist stage, again a natural, though awkward step vis-a-vis the Black Panthers, the Brown Berets, etc. Feminism was also the driving force behind John Rowan's involvement in the men's liberation movement. His *The Horned God, Feminism and Men in Wounding and Healing*, published in 1987, is a personal account of his journey through various political and psychological consciousness-raising groups and is as perfect an historical account as can be found of the individual and collective movement towards liberation among men.

It begins in the early '70s. According to Rowan, the movement began with some anti-patriarchal meetings in the US in 1970. I remember attending a meeting of high school leaders in Norfolk, Virginia in 1968 where the absent father was discussed — in an almost secretive way — but the meeting eventually moved on to such secondary subjects as abuse of authority and war-mongering. The first magazine oriented to the movement was *Brother*, published in 1971 in San Francisco. The movement in Britain, Rowan's home, began in 1972 with a meeting in London, where the men had a hard time deciding how to align themselves with the most radical feminists. One of the suggested names was Unbecoming Men — a nice pun, as well as a telling trait of one of the first steps in liberation, self-denial. These early groups wanted to continue the trends of the gloried '60s and its fabled unshackling of all inhibitive, social-caste balls and chains.

The basic trend was, of course, rebellion against a seemingly insane father and equally, though less vocally and consciously recognized, crazed subjugate mother. The white man, "The Man," the "Great White Father in Washington," represented all that was repugnant in human beings; the mother, all that was to be praised — or saved. The child was the deified promise of a natural being and a pure extension of the enslaved mother. And, in the heady days of youth power the child seemed to be the only force capable of liberating humanity from its madness, of committing the mythic patricide, Isaac taking vengeance.

Of course, to keep oneself from imminent death when one is surrounded by such an omnipotent enemy, it is wise to take on a disguise and what better way than to look almost like the enemy? Almost because you also wanted to look like the liberator. It was a dicey dilemma that resulted in women who looked like girls who looked like long-haired boys.

But what if you were the enemy, or the enemy in the making? What could you be that wasn't what you were to become? Now, exactly what The Man was is still debatable and therefore, so is the rejection of His values. Indeed, one of the most important aspects of the feminist movement was clinical research into the anthropological, social and psychological criteria used to determine the nature of femininity and masculinity. Much of the early work on masculinity was done in the reflected light of the feminist movement. More recently, the question of what it is to be a man has received the specific clinical attention it deserves, and some of this work has made an impact on the larger culture; classes on men's issues are available in colleges and universities around the country. Even good-natured jokes are being made about male feelings on such macho embracing/debunking television shows as *Coach*. While necessary and even safe in its deflection of emotional issues onto the male-safe world of intellectual speculation, the clinical approach to liberation is generally too slow in its dissemination and too often leads to the easy dismissal of, "But who cares what men do in New Guinea on a full moon." The immediate cultural image of a youth icon, such as John

Lennon in the late '70s raising his son and baking bread, has a much more profound impact on how males view their role than a dozen good books on the empirical effects of patriarchal child-rearing, and that can be proven empirically. Regardless, what the New Man was in the early days of the movement was easily seen on the streets of America and Europe. He was a man who looked like a boy who looked like a girl. He was the soft male described by Robert Bly in *New Age Magazine* in 1982, another milestone of male awareness.

But let's take a step back before we look at the hero phase of the movement and gaze into the shadows. The Man, the enemy, the shadowy villain if you will, looked at the feminist revolution, too, and saw that there were, indeed, some problematic areas of common concern to both men and women, namely divorce and child custody. Thus the old, ugly, sophist paradox of reversism came into play. Reactionary in their approach to liberation, such groups as "Free Men," "Men's Rights, Inc.," and the "National Congress of Men" advocated "equal" treatment of men in cases of divorce and child custody that were often misogynistic and homophobic in both intent and deed. Their effect upon the men's movement is still felt and many feminists often associate the current enlightened movement with the nastier aspects of these rump groups. A common complaint about the men's movement is that men already have power, i.e., the thing that feminists want, so why are the poor babies complaining. It is often difficult for someone who wants a bicycle to listen to a bicycle owner complain about a sore butt and a broken chain. What the reactionary men's groups did was to further that power mongering, insensitive, spoiled-brat image. Naturally, groups such as the National Organization of Men Against Sexism wanted to separate themselves from these unbecoming men, even going so far as to write manifestoes denouncing those groups and swearing that they had and would have nothing to do with the gorillas. That is how that relationship stands today.

The mythopoetic question arises as to how else might one deal with this shadow. After all, the issues they bring up are legitimate. It's really their approach that is abhorrent to spiritual liberationists. Perhaps transforming, embracing these men would be more in the spirit of empowering to nurture than the abusive "my way or the highway," authoritarian approach of the radical masculists and their detractors. Also, these masculists bring light to an ironic bit of softness that belies an often conciliatory, almost patronizing approach many pro-feminists take in dealing with the concept of women while the actual treatment of individual women is really rather shabby.

Indeed, the '70s and most of the '80s were a series of stumbles, of small discoveries, of tentative explorations, of mind-expanding and soul-shattering drug use, of big and little mistakes, and quiet gatherings among those willing to or desperate to begin recovery. And might I offer a hardy thanks to those drugs. Had it not been for them, many of us wouldn't nearly have known how fucked up we really were. It was the recovery groups that supplied most of the impetus to delve into the depths of the cultural detritus that provided the basis for a men's movement. It was these codependency discoveries, especially Bradshaw's dysfunctional theories, as well as such New Age insights as the direct emotional relationship between the individual soul and the universe and the environmental impact such a relationship had on the planet in particular, and other general grasping at faddish straws that was the work of the '70s and '80s. In short, we all wanted a life raft, a Noah's Ark, if you will, for the catastrophic, emotional flooding in which we were drowning.

It was incubation, waiting for the moment for the hero to emerge. The gatherings became a bit larger, more voices were emerging, voices that spoke of direct, visceral pain as opposed to theoretical madness. This was getting interesting. Soon, the media were beginning to take notice, books were being written and sold. The '80s were ending better than they started. Reagan had been the perfect foil. All surface and shine, a knight in a tissue-thin armor of lies, all bluster and bullshit macho, afraid to take the hit. The wake up call revealed a bitter emptiness. Shit, we don't want this, do we? Things picked up.

In the fall of 1989, the *Utne Reader* had a devastating issue that ridiculed the movement, and specifically skewered Shepherd Bliss. Such leaders as John Lee were deeply concerned that the movement might die from such early negative publicity. Actually, it turned out to be a boon. *Utne* had never received such reader response before. And the majority of the letters were in defense of the movement. It proved that bad publicity is good publicity, as long as they spell the name right. But more importantly, it was a step away from the belief in armor, the armor that so many men feel must be there, else they will die from the feelings, from the truth. It was time to come out of the AA meetings and coffee klatches and into the public view. It was time to make the same kind of public displays the Civil Rights movement and the Feminist and Gay movements had made. "Look at me! This is it. This is our response." Aha! Denial ends here. This is where history begins. Fuck the armor; we'll take the hit. We'll take responsibility for ourselves and our actions! Marvin Allen invited the media to his Wildman Gatherings and similar negative reviews followed in the *New York Times* and *Texas Monthly*. There were attempts made within the movement to prevent Allen from doing ABC's *20/20* with Hugh Downs, but he insisted and the show in the spring of this year was a major success.

Allen's courage had vindicated another's earlier willingness to take that hit. In January of 1990, Bill Moyers had introduced a smaller portion of the American public to Robert Bly in *A Gathering of Men*. Bly, the poet and the warrior, is the Hero who had to be produced in the men's movement. It could have been Farrell, or Michael Meade, or James Hillman, or Bliss or Lee or Allen, but it was Bly. He is the one. He is the hero/storyteller who drains the dreaded lake to reveal the wildman. Bly has inspired many of the younger men in the movement and now he plays across the TV sets and magazines in a blaze of armor-piercing interviews and charisma-juiced articles. His *Iron John* has, as of this writing, been on the New York Times' best-seller list for 35 weeks, spending most of the time as the number-one non-fiction book. (While non-fiction is Jungian, it is not clinical, and it is more than a little ironic that one of the breakthroughs for the men's movement involves the adventures of a mythological boy. But again, movements use what tools are available.)

So the movement has a hero who inspires articles in popular magazines and becomes the object for jokes by such hip comedians as Richard Belsen on CBS's Good Sports. Ah, more jokes. When they're making jokes, they're taking you seriously.

History is speeding up.

Jokes. We are learning to take the hit and to fan the flames! This is it! *Entertainment Weekly, Newsweek*. More and more mainstream media sources are covering the movement! Oprah and Phil. We have their attention. We are inculcating the culture. What will we do with it?

The men's movement has held the focus of national attention for two years, now. We must hold this energy that has grown around the various leaders and intensify it. We must dip our individual candles into that flame and bring it home. This taking will not enervate the leaders, rather it will energize them and energize those who must be energized, else the future is not only meaningless, but nonexistent.

For what finally matters is not so much the leaders as the many thousands of individuals who must take a spark of this knowledge bought in the glare of national attention and carry it back into their homes, into their workplaces and into their communities. It matters that we take it into these smaller worlds and make it a part of the everyday, mundane environment, that we instill in the culture the power to nurture, that we make such knowledge so deep-seated that we would no more think of life without it than we would think African-Americans are not human or that women are incapable of rational thought.

We must battle the fear of the cult of personality that some say Bly represents by our willingness to take the hit, to question our deeper motives and those who would speak for us. This is the future that matters. It matters that we not become defensive, it matters that we continue to draw attention to the pain in a public way. While we must continue the small, anonymous meetings to share strategies and tactics, to encourage and embolden and nurture ourselves in the battle, in the dance that is life, we must stay at the barricades, tearing them down. It matters for our sons and daughters that we all become heroes, that we all come to know that our history has brought us here to serve.

This is it. This is the place. This is the stepping off place. The dog of the past at our heels, the baggage and treasures of our learning on our shoulders, heaven in our eyes; this is the place. This is the pond of danger, our 15 minutes to decide whether to drain the lake or to watch it evaporate in a slow death waltz. This must be the place where we buried our future. I recognize the roots of the tree of knowledge and the tree of life, or liberation and responsibility. Don't you, Adam?

Masculinity, Society and the Vengeful God

by James Sniechowski

"Nature blundered badly in designing males," writes social commentator George Will in his *Newsweek* column, "Nature and the Male Sex" (6/17/1991). "Because of neurochemical stuff like testosterone," Will sees males as "not naturally suited to civilization." In comparing men to women, he argues that "men are more likely to play roughly, drive recklessly, fight and assault." He feels that such "aggressive" traits are "no longer adaptive in bureaucratized societies that require conformity to many norms so society must evolve institutional restraints and correctives to make men more civilized than they tend to be." Standing on what he believes to be solid, hormonal grounds, he concludes that "Socialization must contend against biology."

Take a moment and check yourself out. How do you feel when you read what Will has to say about what it means to be male? Your answer will reveal just how you regard the men in your life, and how you regard yourself.

Are males biologically deviant? Are we hopeless because we are "badly designed?" Should we look to civilization to subordinate, restrain and correct us? Or should we just resign ourselves to a kick-ass future of rape, plunder, weekends of football and get the hell on with it?

I am deeply angered by Will's commentary. I am insulted as a man and tired of the arguments that would lump me, and the rest of us with external genitalia, into a foregone category of the genetically aberrant, a group which civilization must somehow confine. What is curious is that Mr. Will is also male. Presumably he has been properly civilized.

If you think he is an extremist or in the minority, think again. George Gilder, another writer who speaks in defense of moral conservatism, describes "the crucial process of civilization (as being) the subordination of male sexual impulses and psychology to the long term horizons of female biology." Why? Because, as Gilder believes, males are nothing less than brutish, interested only in short term gratification. They are inherently violent, destructively competitive and need to be constantly controlled.

Biological conservatives, such as Edward O. Wilson, characterize males as being "hasty, fickle and undiscriminating." Why? Because all that men want to do is maximize their opportunities to make copies of their genes. Furthermore, they have more of a load than do women — sperm to egg ratio — so it's in their hard wiring to disseminate widely.

Consider radical feminist Andrea Dworkin. According to her, "Each man, knowing his own deep-rooted impulse to savagery, presupposes this same impulse in other men and seeks to protect himself from it. The rituals of male sadism over and against the bodies of women are the means by which male aggression is socialized so that a man can associate with other men without the imminent danger of male aggression against his own person." What does Dworkin mean? As she sees it, men beat up on females to prevent being beaten up by our own kind.

London psychotherapist, John Rowan, argues that "All power is first of all female power, and the God can only act by relating to her and being with her. But this God is male without a doubt." Rowan sees men as "safe and usable" only if they remain within the feminine and are made powerful only by her.

There is also the position that masculinity is nothing but a role, a set of defensive behaviors that permit men to cope with their dependence upon and powerlessness in the face of women.

Richard Haddad, a vigorous men's rights proponent, believes that "Women run the show by raising their male children to please them, to protect them, and to crave their praise. They raise their female children to keep men in harness, as they do, by rewarding a man's good behavior by dispensing sexual favors, and by punishing the errant male by withholding sex." So, regardless of how it may appear, men are nothing more than hollow shells containing boys who have learned to obey their mothers — or else.

Finally, the two giants, Freud and Jung, attributed enormous power to the unconscious and that power was explicitly feminine. Jung's male hero, the ego, through his struggles and accomplishments in the world, must separate himself from the fundamental, originating feminine principle — the archetypal mother, and then in death return to her to complete his journey.

Jung's argument is that at the primordial level there is no father, no fundamental, originating, masculine principle — no archetypal father.

Freud wrote that "It is the principal task of culture to defend against nature." What he meant by "nature" was the overwhelming power of instinct, the feminine. He bluntly stated that every man must exert a personal effort not to regress into passivity or femininity. A man must "repudiate femininity" in order to establish and maintain his status as a man.

Surely men are more than just sex and violence. Surely we are more than just an impotence struggling against a great, swallowing oblivion. Surely, being masculine contains some dignity, some power, some value in its own right.

It is essential that the men's movement take leadership in developing a body of feeling, thought, imagery and expression that holds, at its core, a principle and experience of maleness that is powerful, generative, fierce, caring, sensual and sovereign, a foundation of masculine being that will stand co-equal with the feminine as a source of life, identity, meaning and purpose. We must develop a mythology that is unashamed to declare the beauty, strength, wonder and spiritual vision of the masculine. We must protect against the depreciation of maleness; not defensively, from desperation, confusion and the absence of a clear sense of self, but open-heartedly and with staunch resolve, knowing that to be a man is more than just good — that a man is a wondrous being, a revelation of the mystery, authority, creativity, passion and potential of life. It is necessary for each of us to listen without compromise for the sounds and signs from within that, when added to others, will give shape to the urge rising from the collective spirit. If this task seems over-reaching, take heart, we already have some beginning clues to the man who is wanting to emerge.

Two seminal contributors in this area are Robert Moore and Eugene Monick. Moore, in his audio tape, *The Great Self Within*, unreservedly declares that "without befriending your grandiosity, you won't live your life very fully, and you probably won't be much of a man, either." In this statement he identifies the inner motivating force inspiring and supporting our effort. In each one of us there exists a "grandiose, exhibitionistic self organization" and it is present in our psyches from the very beginning. It is the impulse that calls us to move beyond, to extend ourselves into the unknown for the purpose of transforming vision and spirit into our daily bread. Moore exhibits the courage to speak of grandiosity as positive rather than pathological, as a value rather than a curse.

To be sure, he warns against infantile grandiosity, the madness of the omnipotent boy, characterizing it "as the fundamental dynamic of all human evil," and warns that the "grandiose boyking must be sacrificed." If he is not, we will not know our limits and we will be possessed by the delusion that we are gods. But the possibility of responsible, mature grandiosity is also available to us. When we befriend our grandiosity we have the inner permission and conviction to believe in our magnificence, trust our competence, live with comfort from the center of our creativity and honor our connection to the divine.

In addition, Monick in his book, *Phallos: The Sacred Image of the Masculine*, provides the beginnings of structure. He calls it "phallos protos" or patrix, the "subjective authority for a male." He locates it in the psychoid unconscious, a primordial level of being wherein matter and non-matter, physis and psyche, soul and spirit coexist — similar to Einstein's unity of matter and energy. From the perspective of the psychoid unconscious, "what is considered to be only physical can just as well be understood as psyche and vice versa." At that fundamental level of being, patrix, the masculine structure, is as omnipresent and inevitable as the feminine matrix.

The importance of Monick's phallos protos is that it represents a ground of being from which men arise and to which they return at death. It establishes the primacy, coequality and spiritual legitimacy of male being. It gives fundamental meaning to a man's existence as a man. It is fecund, life-affirming and expressive. It is beautiful, powerful and expressive. It allows men to look to a masculine source for their reconnection with the erotic, earthy, nurturing and receptive without resorting to the feminine as the only expression of those qualities, an action that makes emotional demands of women that they cannot possibly satisfy. It is an image that can counter the psychological and historical unbalance of solar masculinity, the distant and overbearing sky-father who is rigid, dominant and war-making, chronically involved in sustaining the patriarchal attitude as a way of repudiating the feminine in defense of an unsupported sense of masculine identity.

It is not as though images of earth-based masculine deities have not existed in human culture. Dumuzi, a Sumerian god, husbanded the earth, shepherded the flocks and was a wild, juicy lover. Enki, from Sumer, and Hermes, from Greece, were fluid, magical travelers to the underworld. From Africa comes Ellegua, a phallic trickster god and Obatala, "an androgynous creator God from the Yoruba tradition." From Egypt comes Osiris, whose overflowing fertility brought ripe, full harvest to his people. Judeo-Christianity has no such bountiful, teeming, earthy gods.

Our gods are distant, heavenly, inaccessible, disembodied, capricious, wrathful and have little respect for the feminine.

To be sure, any talk of a masculinity that is loamy, moist and erect will be met with resistance. The vindictive god that dwells on remote mountain tops, or occupies his throne beyond the seventh heaven does not take lightly to any sharing of authority. The institutions belong to him. The armies are his. Religions, philosophies, poetry and commerce pay tithes to his overlording presence. His way is either/or, obedience or death, and we all know just how brutal he can be. Nevertheless, if the men's movement is to contribute to a world that can be whole and hearty, it must assume leadership in moving beyond the old god in search for the new that clearly wants to be born.

It is curious that the men's movement is emerging at a time of rising conservatism. Indicative of this shift in perspective are the events taking place at the United States Supreme Court. The justices have recently handed down a number of decisions that have either repealed or undercut established constitutional rights. One example is the case of Arizona vs. Fulminante in which the Court characterized as merely a "harmless error" the police beating of a criminal defendant in order to extract a confession. Whatever the legal arguments may have been, that conclusion reflects the attitude of an intolerant and merciless god.

The possibility of a woman's right to an abortion being overruled by the high court suggests the absence of respect for women by an invasive and possessive god.

The change at the Supreme Court toward a literalist interpretation of the Constitution according to the "original intention" of its creators, suggests a desire to move in a fundamentalist direction, toward absolutist declarations handed down from on high.

What happens at the Court may seem remote and unconnected from what men are doing in the men's movement, but the Court's attitude reflects a shift to the right in the general cultural attitude. Its decisions set the tone for what lower courts and police agencies will do. And, if George Will has his way, we may see his "institutional restraints and correctives" put into place in order to civilize males who, according to him, cannot help but tend toward lawlessness and destruction.

The point of all this is that modern masculinity has had no fertile spiritual ground upon which to stand, and that fact is now manifested socially as an overt disregard for the value of male being.

Those of us in the men's movement are accountable on two fronts. We must take great care to receive and foster the impulses and images that rise from within. And we must take action that moves us into the world. If we become too heavily focused on our interior life we will invite disaster, as James Hillman argues, "by removing the soul from the world and not recognizing that the soul is in the world." The masculine soul is not only in the world, it is of the world as well.

However, if our action in the world is not rooted in a reliable and steadfast inner ground, whatever we do will be imitation and cliché, sterile and treacherous.

The masculine self is an expression of both an internal principle and a reflection of the community. We cannot have one without the other. Any evolution in the meaning of the masculine self must necessarily be founded upon inner structures expressed through action in, of and for the world.

We men have a responsibility to our local and global culture, and to our time in history and the needs of the future. As is often said, we must become stewards — of ourselves as men, of our children and of the life of this planet. We must stand whole, as men, not badly designed, but aware and accepting of the full range of our potential. We must not repudiate the feminine in order to be men and we must not depend upon the feminine for the connectedness we so desperately long for and require.

Men are assertive and productive, capable of fighting and dying if necessary. Men are also capable of deep connectedness, of loving care, of dedicated nurturing, of all the qualities that have traditionally been attributed to the feminine. However, and this point is critical, we are capable of such as men. Foundational phallos is generative. It stands alongside the archetypal feminine matrix as a source, as sustenance, and as a final ground.

There are those who will agree with George Will, and they will cite history as evidence of the depravity of the masculine. No doubt, history tells a dark tale. However, the men I know and work with, and the man that I am, we all of us know something different — that there is movement deep within male being. A new masculinity is calling out to be born. Its scope is spiritual and political, mystical and practical. Its way is upsetting and careful, nurturing and able to prune. It requires that we have patience and sensitivity to steward it forth, diligence and tenacity to sustain its life. And as we do, the face of masculinity will be remade and the world will be changed in its sway.

Feminism, Men's Rights and the Inner Male:
An Interview with Bob Brannon,
Herb Goldberg and Warren Farrell
by James Sniechowski

With the presentation of the interview between Bill Moyers and Robert Bly, *A Gathering of Men*, a powerful and hopeful response has burst forth around the country. On a scale never before witnessed, men are giving voice to their desire for personal and social change. They are revealing a willingness to accept responsibility for the crippling condition of much of their lives, and, more so, to do the work needed to bring about the changes that will lead to more creative and fulfilling lives as men. A men's movement seems to be under way.

But these developments have not happened overnight. For at least 15 years, some men have been thinking and writing about men's issues. They have been deeply involved with ideas of male role expectations, the relationships between men and women, and the psychology of men. They have helped fertilize the ground in preparation for the growth we are seeing today. And they can rightly be called the early "fathers" of the men's movement.

Recently, I had the welcomed opportunity to interview separately three men who have had a powerful impact on men during the last 15 years: Herb Goldberg, Bob Brannon and Warren Farrell. In talking with them, I found men with thoughtful and seasoned points of view on the issues men face today. Each one brought to our discussions a spirited enthusiasm for communicating what they believe. They did, however, express fundamental differences on the issues men are facing today.

Bob Brannon, from Brooklyn, co-editor of *The Forty-Nine Percent Majority* (1976), views himself as a feminist scholar. Warren Farrell, noted for his books *The Liberated Man* (1975), *Why Men Are The Way They Are* (1986) and *The Ten Greatest Myths About Men* (to be published in 1992), had a 10-year background as a male feminist, but now considers himself a gender futurist. Herb Goldberg, from Los Angeles, author of

The Hazards of Being Male (1976), *The New Male* (1979) and *The Inner Male* (1987), and his new book, *What Men Really Want* (1991), derives his understanding of men from his practice as a clinical psychologist. These men are richly experienced, committed, straightforward and honest. I found them to be sincere, dedicated and open to the pains and joys of what it means to be a man today.

Since my discussion with each man covered the same basic territory, with their cooperation I have organized their responses in the form of a single interview. The result provides an emphasis on the men's movement and an exploration of some of the issues men face today.

I began by asking, "Is there such a thing as the men's movement?"

Brannon: There are several men's movements. The anti-sexist men's movement was the first, I believe, and for a number of years was really all there was. We began about 1970, working from a feminist awareness and a gay-affirmative perspective as well. The part that was slower in developing was how we men ourselves were being harmed by the traditional male role. Within a few years, however, we worked out the sex-role analysis, applying feminism to men's lives. In addition to the anti-sexist men's movement, there are also, of course, those who speak for men's rights, divorced fathers' rights, and then those in the mythopoetic tradition.

Farrell: The men's movement is in its embryonic stage. It is conceived, but unborn. The elements are in place for it to be born during the '90s, but it will take the entire 21st century to mature — because we are talking about a major evolutionary change. Meaning that for millions of years, women selected for the warrior — men who would be willing to die to protect women, children and the community. "Hero" comes from the Greek "ser-ow," from which we get our words "servant," "slave" and "protector."

During those millennia, selecting for the best killer meant selecting for the best protector — killing led to survival of the fittest. But with nuclear technology, selecting for killers leads to the destruction of everyone, which means our genetic heritage is in conflict with our genetic future. That's why we are talking about a fundamental evolutionary change. The men's movement must succeed in getting men to stop being women's protectors — to stop taking the hazardous jobs, earning more money, dying more in war — to stop being the "killer-protector class."

If we don't succeed, we are doubtless talking about the end of our species. We have our work cut out for us to significantly alter this ingrained behavior in less than a century.

Goldberg: Politically, no. But I do think there is a men's movement at the level of consciousness. To me, a men's movement is a symbolic phenomenon, one that says men are exploring their experience and are becoming more conscious of their roles and what their roles do to them personally. More and more men are now working to create a congenial atmosphere in which personal growth can take place. I don't see it as political, though there are some issues. But the political issues are really minor compared to the massive effort and focus required to re-balance a social conditioning that has all but eradicated most men's capacities for personal relationships. If it is perceived as a political movement, there is the real danger and likelihood that some men would exploit the unhappiness of other men and turn false issues into a business. If that happens, the men's movement will become just another hustle.

Sniechowski: What are your feelings about men's rights and those who consider themselves working in the men's rights movement?

Farrell: In the long run, we need a Gender Transition Movement — not a woman's rights movement or a men's rights movement. Right now, though, we need a men's rights movement to create the options for men that women have generated for themselves in the past quarter century.

The focus on fathers' rights in the men's rights movement is politically propitious because almost all movements that have a major impact have large numbers of people who are experiencing emotional rejection and economic hurt at the same time. Just as blacks felt emotionally rejected — "Sit in the back of the bus" — and economically hurt, so divorced fathers often feel emotionally rejected — by being deprived of both their wife and children after divorce — and economically hurt — by paying for children they don't see — the men's rights version of "taxation without representation".

"Equal children for equal pay" is the men's rights equivalent of "equal pay for equal work." Just as women have been supported in the workplace by an Equal Employment Opportunity Commission, men will need support in the homeplace from an Equal Family Opportunity Commission, guaranteeing them as much opportunity to have their children as their ex-wives currently have.

Brannon: When the men's rights groups appeared, they were understandably confused, by some people, with our movement. They were reading our books, having men's groups, calling each other "brother," hugging, getting in touch with their emotions. Superficially, they looked a lot like what we're doing.

But their hostility to women generally and to feminism especially creates a fundamental difference. It means that, at the level of the great moral struggle going around the country regarding gender, in which we side with the victims, they're on the side of the status quo, and holding on to male power.

We've been very clear recently that they're not the same movement as us — that they are part of the problem, not part of the answer. They're co-opting some of the ideas that we've developed and tying them to this very unacceptable holding-on to male privilege.

Goldberg: I don't know what men's rights are beyond a limited point that could best be handled by hiring a sympathetic attorney. To me, "men's rights" implies a kind of activism which implies that men are somehow being done in by society. Their rights are being denied or abused. To outsiders that sounds a little like a joke. Because on a political level, men typically have the power. So, if they are being denied their rights, they've been doing it to themselves. Besides, men's problems, as I see them, are personal, not political.

Furthermore, emphasizing men's rights as the central focus will create the same blind spot present in many feminists where there is a kind of blaming paranoia. If a man begins to see himself as a victim of society and shifts his focus in that direction, he is going to corner himself. Sure, there are injustices men suffer — custody laws, for example. But for men to effect real change, they need to focus on changing their personal selves, which will then lessen the likelihood of personal disasters befalling them.

Sniechowski: Herb, you have said that you see masculinity as a set of defenses. Can you explain?

Goldberg: Masculinity is a set of unconscious defenses. When you put all those defenses together in a man, you have a heavily externalized, performance-oriented, non-personal, disconnected person.

His masculine defenses block fear, vulnerability, dependency and non-mechanical relating. He analyzes to defend against emotion. All his defenses together combine to create a pattern of unconscious disconnection that makes him feel like a man and at the same time makes him incapable of the process of personal connection.

Ordinarily, men have an unconscious identification with their mothers and very little unconscious connection to their fathers in a positive way. In fact, they are repelled by their fathers, who are experienced as cold and distant, punitive and critical. Masculine defenses are in place to protect him from a conscious awareness of his deep fusion with his mother.

Sniechowski: Bob, I know you hold the position that "men only" events are unacceptable, particularly if they are advertised that way. Can you explain why?

Brannon: Perhaps as men we do need time to just be with other men, to talk just with other men. I've done that at informal men's weekends and in a men's group I belonged to for six years. But there's a more important issue than what we want or need, and that's our responsibility to not discriminate.

Martin Luther King talked about how someone looks at the color of your skin and not the quality of your heart and mind, and then decides what you can or can't do or be, based on something you cannot control. I think that transfers quite well to gender.

When men say they need to meet with one another, and that women may not attend, at that point they're wrong. I don't believe it's a wise idea to ever hold meetings that are "for men only."

To achieve what men want by excluding women is an idea I will stand against. It's not just an issue of men's being together, but one of means versus ends. It's not very different from having an event that is open to the public except for people who are black or Jewish. When women are excluded because they are women, how different is it from a "whites only" sign?

Sniechowski: Warren, what do you see as the main issues the men's movement will need to address?

Farrell: The draft and combat; "marrying up"; sharing the risks of sexual rejection; raising consciousness about hazardous jobs and "the 59-cent myth"; men's ABC rights (abortion, adoption, birth, caring); confronting the era of the multi-option woman and the no-option man. These issues are more causal than the "symptom issues" — men dying seven years sooner, being four times as likely to commit suicide, being 24 times as likely to be in prison, being 85 percent of the unsheltered homeless.

First, the draft and combat. There is no law that is more unconstitutional than male-only draft registration. If President Bush said, "As of tomorrow, we will require only Jews to register for the draft," he would be compared to Hitler in his willingness to dispose of Jews. Men are the only group who can be singled out as a group for potential death and be stupid enough to call it "power." We don't understand that throughout history we have been "the disposable sex."

But male-only draft registration is only symbolic of men who join the Army having the obligation to enter combat if needed, while women are protected from entering combat. Pretty soon that will change to women having the option of joining combat, and everyone will call that equality. But it won't be equality until both sexes have the option or both sexes have the obligation. Right now, a quarter of a million women who are protected from combat have forced a quarter of a million men who used to be trained for non-combat positions into combat positions.

The draft and combat are important issues because they are so symbolic of men's protector instinct — of feeling the pressure to earn enough money to protect women to such a degree that when a successful man and woman marry and consider having children, the woman contemplates three options:

1) work full-time

2) children full-time

3) some combination of work and children.

The man allows himself three "slightly different" options:

1) work full-time

2) work full-time

3) work full-time.

Our protector instinct has just evolved from making a killing in war to "making a killing" on Wall Street. Or, among working class men, feeling the pressure to earn enough money to support their families that they end up taking 98 percent of the hazardous jobs—the "death professions"—in order to get the "death professions pay bonus." Drafting only men is also a symbol of our double standard about violence. Violence against women we protest; violence against men we call "entertainment" — westerns, war movies, boxing, football, wrestling, etc.

Perhaps the toughest issue for men to confront will be our feelings of being unworthy of women until we pay for them — whether it's picking up the check after our first dinner together or our willingness to question why a man will marry a woman who is a secretary but not feel very eligible himself if he were a secretary. Once we confront this issue, we see that almost no woman marries a man unless he either earns more than she or she believes he has "potential." She may have sex with him, she may live with him, but statistically speaking she almost never marries him. This means men are not equal until we earn more than women — and that's one of the reasons we're willing to take jobs that pay more, which we like less and that kill us sooner. This is not power, but compensation for powerlessness. Power is not possessed by those who earn the money, but by those who spend the money. Power is not money or status; power is control over our own lives.

I'm going on too long here, so I'll have to let the issues of sharing risks of sexual rejection be read in *Why Men Are The Way They Are* and let the issues of the 59-cent Myth, Men's ABC rights, and confronting the issue of the multi-option woman and the no-option man go until *The Ten Greatest Myths About Men* comes out next year. Suffice to say that all this is but the tip of the iceberg — things I never saw when I was on the board of directors of the National Organization for Women in New York City.

Sniechowski: How do you see the '90s with regard to men?

Goldberg: I think there will continue to be two types of men. One will be the technological man, who will continue to be heavily externalized. More and more of these men will hit the wall. They will become finer and more adept achievers, but at the same time they will become incapable of anything personal. And that will start to become very painful, too painful, in fact, and unconsciously they will self-destruct.

There will also be those men who will work to learn to become more personal and to live in a less externally driven way. However, they will also be in danger. Those men who are striving to become more personal must be alert to the desperate hunger of those who want power and will exploit and take advantage of them. Unilateral liberation is not healthy without an awareness of the total reality. Whereas I used to feel we were all heading for a much better time, I no longer am feeling as optimistic.

Brannon: At the level of sex-role awareness and change, there are some good trends going on. Many young people are understanding the ways men can have richer and better lives by unlearning the traditional male sex role, and the ways in which women can have better lives by unlearning some of the constraints of femininity. The inequality of power between men and women, however, still needs to be addressed.

The "politics of macho" that currently wins national elections is the last hurrah of an old perspective that is clearly being eroded. I see a growing acceptance of homosexuality and feminism among students.

That my female students all expect to have careers, for example, is a solid addition to the cultural mindset. Forty years from now, these changes will have a large impact. People don't laugh anymore when they hear about the oppression of other groups.

I want to see bridges built between the various branches of the men's movement, but not to be co-opted by someone who is working against what I believe in.

Farrell: I see the '90s as the decade the men's movement will be born — but just born. Its birth will create the eruption of millions of "male volcanoes" — the expression of feelings by men who have had to "stuff" their experience as a man because their experience wasn't politically correct. We will redefine power and dominance until we understand that men are not and never have been the powerful or the dominant sex — but that both sexes have been powerful and dominant in their areas of responsibility. We will see that we have been not a sexist world, but a bi-sexist world.

One of the greatest achievements of the 21st century will be a men's movement — ultimately a gender-transition movement — that will see the feminist monologue evolve into a two-sex dialogue, which will ultimately free us to move from Stage I of human history, in which survival was best served by men dying in the process of killing and protecting, to Stage II, in which survival is best served by genuine understanding, mutual listening and therefore a redefinition of love. But accomplishing this will take a new type of guts — a new man.

Sniechowski: Gentlemen, I believe it is vital for all the branches of the men's movement to build bridges to one another. We need to explore mythology, to understand male psychology, to vocalize our experience politically; and we need to embrace women in our redefining what it means to be a man.

Furthermore, I believe we must do everything we can to protect against partisanship. If not, we will lose sight of the fact that the issues we face are about being men and we will become lost in defending positions, excluding differences, name-calling and paranoia.

Each branch has value to contribute. The point, after all, is to become whole men — strong, centered, open, fierce, tender, connected, well-defined and yet willing to discover the future.

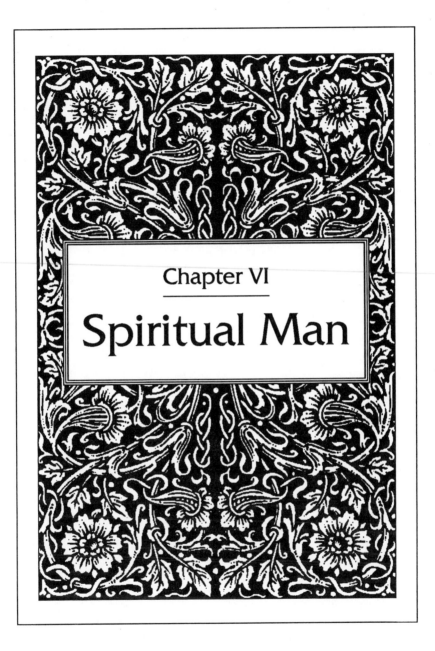

Chapter VI

Spiritual Man

Recovering the Deep Masculine:
The Mythopoetic Approach to Men
by Shepherd Bliss

"Fight to recover what has been lost," T.S. Eliot writes in *Four Quartets*. What is it that has been lost? The deep masculine, many of us believe, is a major portion of our humanity that our culture has lost. Lost but not destroyed. The memories of both men and women, in what poet W.B. Yeats calls The Great Memory, contain remnants of that masculinity. The time has arrived to discover and recover, to create and reclaim masculine modes that are life-enhancing for men, women, children and the earth.

Much has been written about the masculine — by psychologists like Carl Jung, by anthropologists such as Margaret Meade, by poets and novelists such as Walt Whitman and D.H. Lawrence. They have found that the masculine can be many things — deep or shallow; positive or negative; partial or whole; infantile, youthful, mature, or wise. We are all familiar with shallow, negative masculinity. We are less attuned to the deep masculine. How do we discover it so that it might grow more healthy and crowd out the weedy masculinities that have grown in our garden and threatened all of us and our earth?

"Dig deeper," Nikos Kazantzakis encourages, asking, "What do you see?" As he digs within, Kazantzakis discovers the masculine that he writes so beautifully about in *Zorba the Greek* and *Saint Francis*. In one passage, he writes, "I hear voices and weeping. I hear the flutter of wings on the other shore." Then he discovers, "They are not on the other shore. The voices, the weeping, the wings are your own heart." The deep masculine is in the hearts of men and women everywhere, which is why men have drummed for centuries: the heartbeat, the human pulse, the beginning point.

In that heartbeat, we find that the deep masculine is nurturing, playful, forceful and zany. We discover ancient images of men — the moist Egyptian Osiris, who nurtured the earth; the communicative Greek Hermes, who embodied the playful, stealing his older brother's cows soon after his birth; the strong King Arthur's positive power at the Round Table; and the wild Pan's forest zaniness. Osiris in the water, Hermes' fleetness of foot, Arthur's sword, Pan's animalness are all masculinities worth affirming and working to restore.

When I lead men's gatherings outside the United States, I discover different modes of masculinity than those most of us experience in the day-to-day city lives. Recently in Spain, for example, I noted men playing a bowling kind of game in the streets after the noon meal, having great fun, as if they were boys — an unfamiliar sight for goal-oriented U.S. males in the middle of the work day. European men of certain classes greet each other by kissing on the cheeks. In the Basque region, men have a custom of gathering on Sundays to cook for each other. Such forms of masculinity are more social and cooperative than the isolated and competitive masculinity that dominates the United States.

In the more sparsely populated Canada, with almost as much land as the US and fewer people than my home state of California, some men seem to retain the cooperative, rural impulse of harvesting food together, raising barns and volunteering to fight fires. The masculinities I observed in the prairie province of Alberta, representative of positive masculinities one can find throughout rural America, appeared more connected to the earth than the corporate masculinities which prevail in US cities.

The relationship of the masculine to the feminine is often conceived as polar or contrary; we speak of the "opposite sex." Yet relations between the sexes are essentially multifaceted and dynamic, not dualistic and static. Rather than being mutually exclusive, masculinity and femininity can be inclusive, as Jung indicated. Rather than play into what archetypical psychologist James Hillman calls "the fantasy of opposites," we can see masculinity and femininity can be mutually evocative — stimulating the other, rather than combating it.

One day at a skating rink, I watched a skater move forcefully and deliberately toward me. "Such power, how masculine," I thought. A few minutes later, another skater glided toward me, and I reflected, "Such beauty, such grace, how feminine." When the skater passed again, I realized these two images were the same person — at once masculine and feminine. Either/or does not capture the relationship of the masculine to the feminine. Both/and is more accurate.

Night and day are different, yet they are two versions of the same. Mountain and valley, moon and sun, likewise can be seen as contrary or as connected. The masculine and the feminine imply and require the other. The masculine, I know, desires the feminine. The feminine, I feel, desires the masculine. They reach toward the other — sometimes in pursuit, other times haltingly, often nowadays awkwardly. The essence of the phallus is that it connects — reaching out in mysterious ways toward the other. A danger of our language is that it can trap us in contraries. Living things tend to be blended — more gray than white or black.

Ancient images of love in various cultures are often masculine: Eros, Cupid, Frey, Adonis, Tammuz. Hillman notes, "The eros principle is active and aimed." He adds, "Love is male deed and power." The masculine seems to move forward, toward objects, often in pursuit. The masculine tends toward the bright, the outer, the erect, the focused, the conscious, the differentiated. It can lead to individuality and what Jung calls individuation.

When I think of the deep masculine, three clear archetypes emerge:

The Earth Father — such as Johnny Appleseed, who seeds the earth that creativity may continue.

The Husband, who cares for the land and household, who uses resources judiciously and manages prudently.

The Uncle, who helps, advises and encourages.

We need more such Earth Fathers, Husbands and Uncles — men in relation to themselves, nature and others.

The deep masculine cannot be understood without exploring the dark masculine. That which is dark is not necessarily negative. Understanding the masculine requires going beyond rational, scientific thinking. Beyond even psychological thinking, there is what might be called metaphorical thinking or mythopoetic thinking, which is suggestive and generative rather than precise and logical. Mythopoesis is the making of myth; we need to re-mythologize masculinity, returning to the old stories of what it means to be a man.

Hades represents the dark masculine. He is the Greek god of the underworld, the depths, the realm of souls. He lives next to the house of dreams. Sometimes, Hades pulls us down without our consent. According to feminist scholar Christine Downing in *The Goddess: Mythological Images of the Feminine*, the Greek underworld ". . .is not terrible and horrifying, full of punishment and torture, but simply, beyond life." But what is "beyond life?" How can we even imagine it? Words surely escape us. Metaphors, myths, poems and stories help with their powers of evocation.

Downing's chapter, "Persephone in Hades," shows the importance of symbolic thinking over literal thinking. Persephone was abducted by Hades, taken from her mother, Demeter, into the underworld. After deep study, Downing writes, "I began to see Hades as meaning not 'bad,' but 'deep.' " Downing grows beyond a literal interpretation of his act when she notes,

"Persephone gives herself to Hades." Downing herself comes ". . .to recognize how much in me. . . yearned for the depths that Hades represents."

The dance between Persephone and Hades is an intriguing one. It is not that Hades simply takes and Persephone resists. As Downing notes, "The myth captures the ambivalence of the maiden's relation to sexuality (I would add masculinity) as I myself remember it — she reaches out and is taken, the lover is deeply familiar and a stranger." So Hades both "took me from myself" and "gave me to myself" — a power that the masculine has.

If Persephone is to grow, she must separate from her mother. Hades helps Persephone separate from Demeter, which Downing notes is "an experience which was at the same time loss of mother and gain of self." Hades initiates Persephone. In the rational, non-mythological world, we would prefer that this happen with consent and gentleness. Yet those actions beyond our control are often those that lead us to the deepest places.

The masculine, of course, does not have a corner on the world of darkness and its creativity. The dark feminine is embodied by Hinduism in the goddess Kali, whom mythologist Joseph Campbell describes as the "terrible one," who ". . .is represented with her long tongue lolling to lick up the lives and blood of her children. She is the very pattern of the sow that eats her farrow, the cannibal ogress" surrounded by skulls. The dark, feminine Kali and the dark, masculine Hades represent similar mythological places.

Paths to the deep masculine are multiple, and may take one into one's soul or through the outside world with men and women, art and nature. One path is the growing mythopoetic men's movement, which draws men together to restore the lost male community. Seeking to help each other, women and children, these men seek to connect with their boyhoods and emerging as wise, old men. Sometimes, they join women on their journeys.

Such men allow deep feelings to emerge and be expressed. Rather than deny their sadness and grief, they open to it. Ceremonial arts, such as chanting, drumming and dancing can give expression to those feelings. Regaining contact with one's boyhood and sense of play is crucial in this process. Doing so makes a man's life more than work, production and responsibility. The Spanish poet, Federico Garcia Lorca, longs for continuing contact with the creativity of his inner boy: "Give me back / the soul I had as a child, / matured by fairy tales, with its hat of feathers / and its wooden sword."

The mythopoetic men's movement also helps men to regain their ties to nature. Forest, ponds and other natural environments provide space for the deep masculinity to emerge.

Another facet of masculinity that has been recovered by the mythopoetic movement is the male soul's longing for expression in movement and sound. In our work, I encourage each man to practice a physical discipline and play a musical instrument as the expression of his unique soul. The movement can be the swiftness of running or the grace of Tai Chi. Thoreau's physical path included walking each afternoon. The New England centenarian Scott Nearing built stone homes and cut firewood into his nineties. Thoreau listened to birds and played the flute. Francis of Assisi played a stringed instrument similar to the mandolin. The sound can be the deep tones of the huaca flute that my fireman friend, Ray Gatchalian, plays or the exuberance of the gongas that my partner, Bruce Silverman, plays. There are many physical paths and many musical sounds that evoke the deep masculine.

Wholeness on the
Wings of Spirit
by David Kramer

We know that a wounded man, a man who is missing essential parts of himself, needs a healing towards wholeness. He needs to retouch his anger and his grief, regain communion with his body and receive intimacy and love. Yet a man needs more than a wholeness that is a rebuilding and restructuring, as terribly crucial as this is. A man needs a wholeness that is also a purification and a transcendence; a man needs spirit. A wounded man must take some of his substance, that which he has reclaimed and healed, and purify it and transform it into a spiritual light and a spiritual lightness that allows him to fly up among the mountain peaks and beyond, into the sky. That is the healing for which a wounded man, a wounded human being, must strive: a wholeness of the soul that is purified for flight on the wings of the spirit.

However, we do not, and especially men do not, acknowledge the power of spirit. We do not, as a general rule, even acknowledge its existence. Our rationally trained and empirically needy minds can make no room for it within their narrow view of reality. Our denial does not rid us of spirit but, as Grimm's fairy tale, "The Spirit in the Bottle" shows, only turns spirit negative and destructive. The story demonstrates that if we can overcome this initial obstinacy of the mind, this initial fear, and open ourselves to the spirit, we can find the places in our being where spirit is born, nurtured and taught to fly.

The Grimm brothers' tale begins like this: a boy comes to a dangerous-looking oak that is many hundreds of years old, and says, "This looks like a good place for birds' nests." No sooner does he start looking than he hears a smothered voice, crying for liberation: "Let me out, let me out!" He looks around and digs the earth among the roots until at last he finds a glass bottle buried in the ground. The boy uncorks the bottle and immediately a spirit ascends out of it until the spirit is almost twice as big as the oak tree. The spirit cries, "I am the mighty Mercurius. I must strangle whomever releases me." The boy is shocked by this response and stalls for time, trying to think of something to say. Finally, this: "Oh, Mighty Mercurius, if you are so powerful and so smart, let me see if you can get yourself back into that little bottle. Then I will believe in you and I will be in your power." In response to this challenge, Mercurius makes himself small and goes back into the bottle. The boy quickly corks the bottle and throws it back in among the roots of the old oak tree.

For most men in our culture, the story stops here. The boy merely returns to his woodcutting and becomes a woodcutter or returns to his school and becomes a scholar. Without spirit flowing into his life, there is a vacuum, and this vacuum is most often filled by an abundance of work. Sooner or later, work will "cure" his desire to fly. Indeed, it has been said that work is the Jungian cure for the "infantilism" of the *puer aeternus*.

Bottling the spirit back up and walking away from it forever is the common sense, practical thing to do. The encounter with the spirit is an extremely dangerous one; its presence is overwhelming and its murderous intent obvious. Anyone who has done even a little digging around the roots and mud of the tree of his being is familiar with the dangerous qualities of the released spirit. In a culture where technology, represented by the bottle, is used to imprison spirit, the liberation of the spirit may well threaten the survival of the liberator. That which has been denied throughout the age of reason in which we have been born is not surprisingly, in a first encounter, nasty, threatening, murderous and evil.

Yet, in a direct contest with the boy's mind, trained at school to think rationally, the spirit is easily defeated. With one of the oldest tricks in the book — a demand that Mercurius distinguish his reality from a normal reality in which a thing cannot grow or shrink at will — the boy is able to trap the spirit in the bottle, throw it away and forget about the whole mess.

It is all too easy.

The same culture that hides Mercurius from us teaches us how to deny him when we find him. We have so thoroughly inundated ourselves with the notion of the omnipotence of our logic and our science that, with no objection at all, we let them "prove" spirit out of existence. We do not know who Mercurius is and we do not know the nature of the power that we deny when we throw him back into the dirt and roots of our beings, but we trick him out of our conscious existence just the same.

But it is not as easy as it looks, for Mercurius knows we are out there and will make himself known.

Mercurius springs from the metal mercury, or quicksilver, the only metal that is a liquid at normal temperatures. Because it is a liquid that does not make the hands wet, it is called "dry water," the first of the infinite number of contradictions that this god contains. Mercurius as fluid contrasts with Mercurius as fire, for the planet Mercury, closest companion of the sun, almost loses itself in the fire of that star. The body of Mercurius is both male and female — he is often shown as the hermaphroditic offspring of the sun and the moon. In his guise as the Greek god Hermes, the messenger of the gods, Mercurius is the mental messenger of spirit—the conscious bridge for a human to think about and perceive spirit. Yet Hermes was also a famous trickster, full of dangerous surprises, and Mercurius also reflects the aspect of the spirit that is out of human control, that leaps out from the unconscious.

It is no wonder that Mercurius wants to strangle his liberator; he is such an overwhelming conglomeration of everything at once that he can be sealed inside a bottle only with great pain. It is the nature of this spirit that he not be compressed; there is barely sufficient room in the entire universe to contain all of his opposites. Carl Jung indicates that it might even be part of Mercurius's contradictory nature to be a disunity as well as a unity; "Mercurius consists of all conceivable opposites. He is thus quite obviously a duality, but is named a unity in spite of the fact that his innumerable contradictions can dramatically fly apart into an equal number of disparate and apparently independent figures." Our mind imprisons Mercurius in the bottle in a false unity of pain and destruction.

There is more here. Even before the more or less conscious perception of the spirit as threatening and the consequent denial of its power and existence, there has been a denial on a deeper, unconscious level. Spirit is a part of us; there is a binding between man and Mercurius, albeit an unconscious one. How else is the boy able to find the spirit and hear its plea to be rescued? The binding is as powerful as the sex drive, or the need to eat, or the urge to power.

A man's denial of this binding with spirit keeps the man a *puer aeternus*. It gnaws at him and cries out to him from the roots of his being. It saps his energy. Unclaimed spirit will not let a man go. It will not let a man go fully into life; it keeps the man from ever making a commitment, it keeps the man's life provisional, until it is allowed to accompany him in the living of that life.

Not only does a negative binding with spirit keep a man from living in the here and now, from engaging in life; it also poisons those in his life whom he most loves. The negative and murderous aspects of the denial of the spirit are projected onto the intimate partner. The embrace of the partner seems, in all truth, to be the enemy of spirit, to be designed to suffocate the spiritual drive upward. A relationship becomes exactly like fly paper. It feels as though it pulls the man down, it clips and fouls his wings. These projections, fueled by the power of the spirit that has been cut off, are forcefully real. The man cannot commit but must run away or destroy the relationship.

These negative projections disappear when a man accepts his deep binding with spirit. The spirit no longer clutches at him; the spirit is him. He soars into manhood, not through a "cure" such as work, but by accepting the fact that he can fly and by practicing, by taking flying lessons. He becomes the eagle that he is.

When a man breaks open the bottle, he can be consumed by the outrush of negatively charged contradictions and complexities, but he can also see the beginning of a true unity of the spirit, a unity of power, and a unity that pours energy into him. He is bound to spirit and although he may run away from it, it will stretch only so far before it holds out an image of its true unity and healing power, with which it hopes to snap him back.

Inevitably, the boy returns to the bottle a second time. It is not the safe thing to do. It does not make sense on a conscious level, but spirit seems to be running the unconscious show. The boy hears the spirit from somewhere in his being calling to him, begging, "Ah, do let me out! Do let me out!" And the boy, acting quite irrationally, yielding to the foolish part of his nature, cannot resist. A compelling part of him, a part below or above his conscious mind, has sensed the power of the true unity of the spirit. He can only gain access to that unity if he is willing to run the risk of losing control of his life. Anything could happen to him — something for which he, his conscious self, might wish or something for which he might not wish. That is the pain of it. That is the point of it.

The price of an encounter with spirit, however, is not that we abandon our logic, but only that we loosen its grip on our lives. In the fairy tale, before opening the bottle for the second time, the boy engages Mercurius in quite a bargaining process. "All right, Mercurius, I have come back, even though I think I must be crazy to be here again. But I'm not going to take the cork out without at least getting you to agree not to strangle me."

"I promise, I promise," says the spirit, "I won't harm you."

"Good," says the boy, "that's a start. But what's in it for me?"

"If you will set me free again," replies the spirit, "I will reward you richly."

The boy puzzles over that one. Well, that's pretty vague," he says. "Can't you be more specific?"

"No," replies the spirit indignantly, "You don't realize how lucky you are to even be talking with me. Take it or leave it."

The boy may throw out a final rationalization, "Well, whatever happens, I can handle it," but he has made his decision. He is wounded and without wings. There is a chance that Mercurius might help him. It is worth risking even his life for this chance.

The help that Mercurius gives, the gift that the boy receives, is the most entrancing part of the story. Mercurius, freed from the bottle for the second time, tells the boy, "Now you will have your reward," and he gives the boy a little bag, just like plaster. If one end of the bag is spread over a wound, the wound is healed. If the other end of the bag is rubbed on steel or iron, it changes the steel or iron into silver.

The plaster bag truly reflects the bundle of opposites that is the personality of Mercurius. "Plaster" comes from the same Greek word from which "plastic" comes; it means a molding, a forming. Plaster is a material that has a substantial degree of fluidity as it is being molded but becomes "fixed in concrete" once it has set. The gift of the bag underscores the provisional nature of the *puer aeternus*, the refusal to commit to a relationship or to life, the insistence on a fluidity of possibilities. At the same time, the bag points to the growth of the *puer aeternus* into a man of the here and now, a "concretized" man.

Mercurius has taken the most mundane material in the world — a bag of little more than mud — and transformed it into the most extraordinary of objects, the Philosopher's Stone that changes base metals into precious ones. The spirit transforms and purifies a substance that in turn is capable of transforming and purifying the world.

The boy puts this transformative power to work immediately. He rubs the bag against the iron axe blade and changes it to silver. He then hefts the axe and chops into a tree; the silver blade bends and does not cut. The father somehow does not see that the blade is silver and is horrified that the boy has ruined the axe.

Here the story takes a penetrating little twist. The father, the side of our nature that represents the collective, the practical point of view, is blind to the value of the transformation and is outraged that the blade has been ruined. It didn't belong to the boy in the first place; it was a neighbor's, and now even more wood will have to be chopped to pay for it! A man who seriously engages the spirit in its transformative aspect must be prepared for this reaction from his society. Not only will those around him not see that he has transformed a part of his reality (the drudgery of work) into precious silver, they may well be horrified at his actions and think that he has made a ruin of things.

In fact, a part of him has ascended. Transforming iron into silver is, for those who can see it, a true flight of the spirit. Symbolically the boy soars to the mountaintops where the untouched snow and the crystalline streams glisten silver in the sunlight. And beyond that to the stars.

A world full of silver axe blades is, however, an incomplete world. The silver gained on the mountaintop must be brought back down into the valley and cashed in.

That is what the boy does. He takes the bent blade to town and uses the money he gets from selling it to return to school. He goes on learning more and, as he can heal wounds with his bag, becomes the most famous doctor in the whole world. And so the fairy tale ends.

The ending is an unusual one. There is no princess to be courted and no kingdom to be won. Instead of settling down to live happily ever after in some obscure castle, the boy goes out and heals the world. It could be speculated that, with his power to transform base metals into silver, he not only heals the world, he makes the world shine. His plaster bag is not the same as most fairy-tale gifts that can be used once, twice, or at the most, three times; the plaster bag keeps its powers forever. The ending of this story points beyond the goal of a wholeness that is happiness or even fulfillment; it points to a wholeness that is the creative and durable power of Mercurius the spirit. A man who has risen on silver wings to the mountain peak and returned to play and heal in the valley of the world's soul and the soul of his being is a creator. His creation becomes his recreation for as long as he lives.

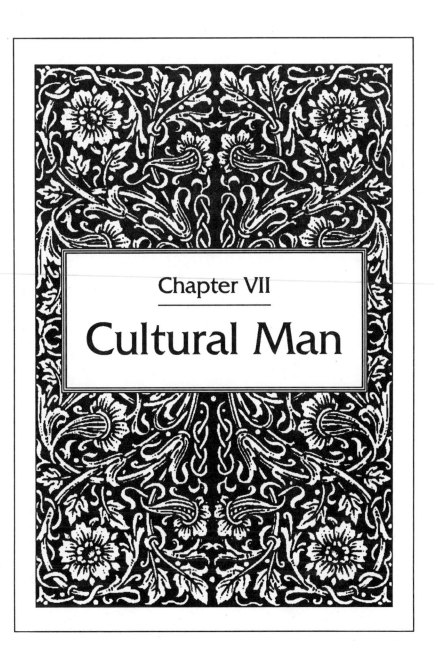

Chapter VII

Cultural Man

An Anthropologist's Journey into Masculinity Studies
by David D. Gilmore

Before I went to Spain in 1972 to do a social-anthropology study, I studied English literature; and like all red-blooded American adolescents, I read bildungsroman novels: Jack London, Ernest Hemingway, Norman Mailer, all that boy-into-man stuff. I confess also that I succumbed to the usual urges and went to Spain to run with the bulls in Pamplona, along with a pack of equally crazed pals. Luckily I survived this episode, but it left some mental residues. I at once noticed that boys in Spain seemed to be preoccupied with displays of manhood — even more so than Americans — but also seemed to have something in their experience that my own culture lacked: a public test or tournament of manhood — a rite of passage — by which they could demonstrate their prowess. In other words, they seemed to have the route to a culturally sanctioned manhood, if not easier, then at least more clearly defined. They knew exactly what they had to do to be an "hombre." It had less to do with violence than courage.

Later in Andalusia for a year's field work, I was constantly bombarded by miscellaneous impressions of a manhood or virility obsession — the need to be called "macho." The word macho comes from the Castilian word for "male," and it has worked its way into many other languages as "machismo," which also attests to the Spanish (and offspring Latin-American) cases being merely exemplars, or somewhat hyper forms, of a widespread sociological phenomenon that is by no means confined to Hispanic cultures.

Despite its Moorish heritage, Spain and even Andalusia are part of a general Western European literary tradition. Most other Westerners, including Americans and Englishmen, have always been concerned with manhood as a matter of personal identity or reputation. This was strong in Elizabethan times, as any reading of Shakespeare will attest. For example, when Lady Macbeth tries to motivate her demoralized husband, she goads him by taunting, "Are you a man?" and the worst insult in Jacobean England was to call a man either "womanly" or a "goodman

135

boy," both ways of impugning his manhood. This sort of thing continues in our own day. Norman Mailer writes: "Masculinity is not something given to you, something you're born with, but something you gain . . . . And you gain it by winning small battles with honor." And of course we have heard similar statements or exhortations in our own experiences. "Act like a man," "be a man," "show what kind of man you are," etc. In the West, manhood is historically an ideal that is contested, achieved, fought over. It does not come easily.

When I returned from Spain in 1973, I had many conversations with colleagues on the subject of these male-gender codes. I found that most other anthropologists had similar experiences. In fact, I had a number of friends who went so far as to use the term "machismo" to describe what they saw in places like Africa, the Middle East, Oceania and Micronesia. So I decided to do some cross-cultural research on the subject, partly because as far as I knew, no other anthropologist had tackled the subject. Most so-called "gender studies" were done by women; the work is mainly about women and for women.

I found some common threads. I found that manhood ideals in the form of passing tests were almost universal, but not quite. I call the manhood phenomenon "ubiquitous" but not universal. What I found is that the concern for manhood as an achieved status is widespread. On Truk Island, a little atoll in the South Pacific, for example, men are virtually obsessed with being masculine. Echoing Lady Macbeth, a common challenge there is, "Are you a man? Come, I will take your life now." In East Africa, young boys from cattle-herding tribes, including the Maasai, Rendille, Jie and Samburu, are taken away from their mothers and subjected to painful circumcision rites by which they become men. If the Samburu boy cries out while his flesh is being cut, if he so much as blinks an eye, he is shamed for life as unworthy of manhood. The Amhara, an Ethiopian tribe, have a passionate belief in masculinity called wand-nat. To show their wand-nat, Amhara youths are forced to engage in bloody whipping contests called buhe. Far away, in the high mountains of Melanesia, young boys undergo similar trials before being admitted into the select club of manhood. They are torn from their mothers and forced to undergo a series of brutal rituals. These include whipping, bloodletting and beating, all of which the boys must endure stoically.

Among Native Americans, or Indians, there are parallels. The Tewa people of New Mexico, for instance, believe that boys must be "made" into men. Tewa boys are taken away from their homes, purified by ritual means, and then whipped mercilessly by the Kachina spirits (their fathers in disguise). Each boy is lashed on the back with a crude yucca whip that draws blood and leaves permanent scars. "You are made a man," the elders tell them afterwards. Girls undergo rites of passage, but without the testing element, without the trials. The Fox People of Iowa call being a man "The Big Impossible," something that only a few can achieve.

Sometimes, as in Andalusia, virility or potency is paramount in these manhood evaluations; elsewhere, as among the Trukese and Amhara, physical toughness is more important. Sometimes economic "go-getting," athletic ability, or heavy drinking are the measures of a man. The ingredients vary, but in all these places a man has to pass some sort of test, measure up, accomplish something. There is a clear distinction made between anatomical maleness, having a penis, and being a "real man."

Manhood is therefore a prize to be won, a critical threshold defined symbolically; it is not conferred by anatomy alone. Hence, there is almost everywhere a parallel negative category of false or phony men. In the Balkans, for example, a grown man must show an "indomitable virility" that distinguishes him from effeminate counterfeits. In Morocco, "true men" are distinguished from "effete men" on the basis of physical prowess and heroic acts of both feuding and sexual potency. Likewise, for the Bedouin of Egypt, "real men" are contrasted to despicable weaklings who are "no men." In New Guinea, real men are contrasted to what are called "rubbish men," who are weak and feminine. Among the Brazilian aborigines, "real men" are distinguished from "trash-yard men," who are said to be timid and soft like women.

Perhaps these colorful manhood invectives seem bizarre to us at first glance. But none of them should surprise most Anglo-Americans, for we too have our manly traditions, both in our popular culture and literary traditions. Although we may choose less flamboyant modes of expression than the Amhara or the Tewa, we too have regarded manhood as an artificial state, a challenge to be overcome, a prize to be won. For example, let us take a people and a social stratum far removed from those above: the gentry of modern England. Among the British upper classes, young boys were traditionally subjected to similar trials on the road to their majority. They were torn at a tender age from mother and home, as in East Africa or in New Guinea, and sent away in age-sets to distant testing grounds that sorely took their measure. These were the public boarding schools like Eton and Rugby, where a cruel trial by ordeal, including physical violence and terrorism by elder males, provided a passage to a social state of manhood which their parents thought could be achieved in no other way. Supposedly, this harsh training prepared young Oxbridge aristocrats for the self-reliance and fortitude needed to run the British Empire, and thereby manufactured a serviceable elite as stylized as Samurai. Even here, in Victorian England, a culture not given over to showy excess, manhood was an artificial product coaxed by austere training and testing.

Yet interestingly, manhood codes are not just a call to aggression. For example, the brutal "machismo" of violent men is not real manhood in any of the cultures I have mentioned, but a meretricious counterfeit — a sign of weakness. A curious commonality is that true manhood is a call to what I have called service-to-society, which is a kind of nurturing or nourishing. I found that "real" men are indeed "nurturing." Real men seem to be those who give their society more than they take, according to some invisible, quantitative calculus; these are men who actually serve others by being brave and protective.

However, this "manly" nurturing is different from the female kind of nurturing. For one thing, it is less direct and more obscure; the "other" involved may be society in general, rather than specific persons. Yet real men do nurture. They do this by shedding their blood, their sweat and their semen to help their society, by bringing home food, by producing children, by dying if necessary in remote places to provide security for their families. From a characterological point of view, this masculine nurturing is paradoxical, because to be supportive, a man must first be tough to ward off enemies; to be generous, he must first be selfish to amass goods; to be tender, he must be aggressive enough to court, seduce and "win" a wife.

All this means that ideals of manhood can have their positive uses. As an anthropologist, I think we need to study such ancient traditions carefully and dispassionately before we decide to get rid of them. The present call among feminists and others to eliminate such role models and distinctions based on sex are premature. Before we jettison all aspects of gender, we should first consider the consequences of eliminating goals, ideals and competitive challenges from our lives. After all, the meaning of our lives and the joys we derive from life are based in part upon personal fulfillment within society. This in turn is based on accomplishing something. But all achievement comes from measuring one's performance against the best; in this way, both we and our society benefit.

Courage and AIDS

by Randolph Severson

I weep for the courage of noble men.
— Robert Duncan

To move among the AIDS afflicted is to be overwhelmed with incredible images of courage, of courage often wordless but palpable. Here are young men — young men once handsome, brilliant, young men in the proverbial prime of life, who only a few years ago were flushed-cheeked and glitter-eyed, their faces shining in the excitement of a sexual and political liberation. The closet door, nailed shut for centuries, swung open to reveal the queens and queers, and the queens and queers were us, a brother, a son, a friend. But now these same young men are corpses, pale and wan, bloodless, skeletal, emaciated, gasping, stricken with sores and hopelessness. And yet, with the glow of promise fading, while the object of fear and scorn, still they endure and strive, meeting that final test of courage that every traditional culture has imposed upon its young men, the final test of dying well. When Montaigne writes that in the "last scene between ourselves and death, there is no more pretense," so that "in judging another man's life, I always inquire how he behaved in the last; and one of the principal aims of my life is to conduct myself well when it ends," he echoes this ancient tradition. The victims of AIDS are dying well, with a courage and composure that Montaigne would have honored.

Do I seem to be glorifying gays? Do I appear to be idealizing an often sordid and promiscuous lifestyle? Let me be clear. I do not wish to exalt every homosexual into a hero, but I am affirming that the courage with which many of these young men are facing death ought to heighten our appreciation for that portion of heroism in being gay, being queer in a hostile culture. Coming out of the closet is probably not so unakin to a novice boxer's coming out of his corner to answer the bell, even when he knows the cost is pain and potential humiliation. Further, it has taken some honest faith and simple courage for gays to attain the kind of social and political legitimacy to which, in recent years, they have succeeded. And now, a plague. Can we not admit that the authority of these experiences, their agony and action, has impressed upon the souls of gays an indelible print of nobility?

It has been ages since we have had such images of young men nobly facing death peddled in our thoroughfares. Ages since we have seen the athlete dying young lodged within our mythic discourse. In search of correspondences by which to gain an insight into AIDS, we have to hearken back to World War I, to the Guns of August and the Quiet on the Western Front, to the trenches and the generals, to all those elegant aesthetes, the heirs of Wilde, wandering in the Wasteland. In the Great War we find the same images that we confront in AIDS: the once-beautiful but now dilapidated bodies; the smashed emblems; the superbia immobilized by shell shock.

The likeness of the AIDS ward to the trenches reminds us that we are still all walking in a Wasteland. The lights in Europe are still all out. The darkness is advancing. And like the bodies of all those beautiful young men shipped back to Paris, London, Berlin and Vienna, AIDS stands as an indictment of all those causes and presumptions that led into the trenches: the materialism, the monotheism, the Satanic mills, the White Man's burden. AIDS condemns as well all our ostensible solutions: the modernism and post-modernism; the Death of God, the anti-heroes; the cybernetics, new physics, structuralism, deconstructivism, feminism, etc. These avenues, say AIDS, lead nowhere, save to more destructively entoil us. If the Wasteland really is to end, we must venture some livelier, more illuminating questions. We need more than a New Age ethic of whistle while you die.

Besides reminding us that courage exists, AIDS reveals courage as a masculine reality. Though not exclusively, of course, it is men who are dying from AIDS. Not women, not children, not the New Age androgyne. It is men who are suffering; men who are trying to pay their bills; keep their air conditioning running; stay bathed; stay fed; stay living. The funerals are for men. It is men who are being carried out by pallbearers wearing gloves. I have often wondered, with others, as to what response would have followed had AIDS first surfaced among women, whether gay or straight. What if it had been young women who, when they had at last come to the Gates of Eden, to their full inheritance of power, had suddenly found their lives cut down, their promise blotted out? Because the image of the young man dying is somehow so perversely tolerable, so appealing, even, it deranges our response, so that all too often it immunizes us against the appalling toll of suffering. If AIDS should really prove to be a man's disease; if the virus should eventually reveal itself to be a spectre haunting only gays, will the money still pour in, the media coverage, the research, the conferences? Will it all be there, agitated and available, even after the Four Horsemen have passed by, and the ancient, anguished, apocalyptic cry of The Plague! The Plague! has faded, and there is nothing left save what was there at first: young men dying, delirious, beleaguered, impossibly alone?

Since AIDS is afflicting primarily homosexuals, we ought especially to spend some time recovering the immense value of *homoeros*, of the soldierly, erotic camaraderie present in all traditional male vocations, the sensual pleasure that men can sometimes take in one another's company, while passing the bottle or the buck. Increasingly among male clients, I find a kind of generalized malaise, an utterly bewildered alienation, that extends its roots into an injured father complex, where the father is untouchable, with no real presence of his body and his blood, a remote and distant Protestant household god who never butted heads or bear-hugged, and thus affirmed a young man's physical reality as a male among other males. We must look again at all male mysteries — the mysteries of court and camp, vision quest, contest and display, hierarchy and logic, and we must consider them mysterious, magical and swashbuckling, with overtones of Stevenson and Scott, a rough terrain ateem with sanities now worthy of fresh articulations.

AIDS teaches us the liaison between courage and youth. Clearly it is the young men who are dying, the young whose bright eyes and unmarked features are blurring and darkening with shadows. It is the image of the young man dying before his time that evokes such pity, terror and occasional revulsion in our hearts. Now, this association of youth with courage extends the classical assumption that courage is a virtue characteristic of youth, whereas the wisdom of old age consists of prudence and forbearance. So both our times and tradition invoke acknowledgement that courage can often coexist with some of the most irksome properties of adolescence: the egoism and belligerence, the materialism, dramatic acting-out, the grandiosity and narcissism — especially the narcissism we need to reconsider along the lines of Aristotle who declares that:

> The good man ought to be a lover of self, since he will
> then act nobly, and so both benefit himself and aid his
> fellow; but the bad man ought not to be a lover of self,
> since he will follow his base passions, and so injure
> both himself and his neighbors.

If narcissism is really on the rise, as every bitter academic tirelessly reminds us, then I am not so certain we should regret it.

Since AIDS is transmitted through the blood and body fluids, we move beyond the Stoic, Lutheran and existentialist conception of courage, which in light of AIDS must now seem to be cold-blooded in its attitudes. The AIDS-inspired idea of courage is less the Roman and more the Celt; less the legionnaire with his watch on the Rhine, and more the Berserk bursting out of timeless forests. AIDS allies courage to what is hot-blooded in our natures; to what is wanton, excitable, impetuous, even overwrought. This is the courage of Alcibiades, of cavalier and conquistador.

Just as Freudians might read history through Eros and Jungians through soul, so Adlerians may give a historical account in terms of courage; for these two views of courage, the somber and the gallant one, have often vied for political and cultural supremacy. They have often crossed swords in the field. It is Celt versus Roman; Elizabeth against Philip; cavalier opposed to roundhead; the Bonnie Prince against the Butcher Boy; the Stars and Bars arrayed against the Stars and Stripes. So perhaps AIDS is calling us to banners in the dust, to memory and to arms, to a renewal of the struggle against a world economic order erected on the grave of chivalry and romance. Contra Burke, perhaps the Age of Chivalry is not dead.

Yet AIDS also affirms the bond between tenderness and courage. This is the tenderness of Barry Skiba, a local AIDS education counselor who, on a last visit to a victim already lost within a coma, chose to comb the patient's hair and splash his favorite cologne about his face because, says Skiba, he was convinced the man could smell it and sense the dignity. By uniting tenderness to courage in the fabric of a single testament, AIDS reminds us that tenderness belongs to masculine life, even when it flourished in its most distinctive forms, such as courage in the trial of strength or the drinking bout. Outside of the embattlements of war, men are rarely so tender with one another as when, following a fight or drinking spree, a friend or stranger is helped up off the floor, his neck rubbed, his back patted, his hair and clothes smoothed out, his legs propped up beneath him so that he may stagger out with some shred of dignity intact, some nobility surviving. Regrettably, however, and with consequences for courage and culture, it is only at such elusively sporadic moments that men apparently can tolerate the expression of such gentle, lyrical affections.

AIDS reveals how courage copes when death comes, not as a bolt from the blue or in a blaze of glory, but through a vicious, gradual decline. Here courage crosses into weariness. This is the weariness of old King Priam in Achilles' camp. It is the weariness of Allen Ginsberg mourning Kerouac and Cassady: "The mood is sadness, dear friends...." Weariness approaches burnout. And we all know what betokens burnout: dry eyes, pinched features, sapped energies, a cindery, bitter, evil taste within the mouth. Teachers, doctors, social workers burn out. So, too, do those destroyed by the pitiless, unflinching grip of terminal disease. We can burn out on our cancer or our AIDS. But weariness is not burnout. It differs; for weariness is burnout unresisted, gone the whole way through, until all personality is purged away to leave nothing but a shadow. But the shadow is the essence. The ashes of burnout become the ashes and dust of an indestructible nature. What was merely going through the motions becomes a revelation of the Eternal Return. All discursive fretting fades away to be subsumed into a mystic silence. Weariness is the lived, heartfelt, bone deep recognition of ancestral curse and burden. It is the realization that what we are doing, whether it be healing or dying, has been done before, done better, by better men, perhaps, but that it still needs doing, doing now, and that we must do it as well as we are able.

Courage has a visible form. So does weariness. It is the form of the statue of the Dying Gaul. Commissioned on the occasion of some nameless victory by some forgotten king, it depicts a young Celt warrior who has fallen on his shield. He is suffering from a chest wound from which he cannot possibly recover. The life and blood is pouring out. The shield is one of the great oval war-shields carried by the Celts. Around him lie other weapons — a sword, a trumpet. The young man is beautiful and naked. He wears nothing but a golden torque. The neck is bent. The head is bowed. He falls rapidly on his last support, a right arm, that will shift and shift, then tremble, then collapse. The Gaul is dying still. In the faces of the AIDS afflicted, I see him. In their dampened, unmade beds, I see his shield; in their agony, his weariness.

Most important, AIDS founds a community on courage. AIDS recovers an ancient law: communities can be founded on courage — not Eros, not soul, not law nor economics nor comfort nor success, but courage. I do not know whether in advance of AIDS a true homosexual community existed. I doubt it. Sexual orientation is not enough. But now, because of AIDS, one definitely is forming. In discovering their courage, gays are discovering community. They are displacing upwards, from genitals to heart. From the first appearance of the virus, the victims of AIDS have been drawn into communities, gathering into groups to contend with desolation. AIDS counselors agree that perhaps the only way to come to terms with AIDS is through some form of group connection. These groups, these communities are of a timeless sort. Sometimes, they are composed of many; more often, two or three. In part, of course, personal and economic needs prod them into being, but they endure and ripen into mystery because of courage. In their midst men find a necessary courage and then embody it for others. The dynamic underpinning them is an ecology of valor. Men elect to live together in shabby apartments, disowned by relatives, or in halfway houses, penned in by angry neighbors; or they keep returning to group therapy when there is nothing left to say and even the therapist is speechless, because there they find some nourishment and inspiration for the courage needed to survive.

Let me illustrate with a story assembled from a local paper. In this case, the community is formed by two. One is Kurt, 26, a bricklayer, a heterosexual who supposes that he picked up the disease from a tattoo needle. He shares a small, inconspicuous, forlorn apartment with his roommate, Daryl, a black man, a former female impersonator who once drove a bus in New York City. In the article I am summarizing, Kurt is pictured ashen-faced, stick-limbed, with a piece of linen wrapped around his forehead, fingering a blanket while he lies on a sofa watching TV. Having at one time boasted the impressive, solid frame of a bricklayer, his weight has plummeted to 80 pounds. His friend, Daryl, is slightly better off, though his lungs are suffering through a second siege of pneumonia. Daryl continues coping while Kurt drifts deeper into the last stages of the disease. The two men live together, an unlikely pair, because they need and want to. There is no one else, no other room to flee to. They talk; they pass the time. They have only their friendship and their vigil. And their courage.

Most of us suppose western civilization to be composed of three great cities: Athens, Jerusalem and Rome. In addition to these, there was another. There was Sparta.

In most accounts of the formation of the western mind, Sparta has been neglected or defamed, as in the word Spartan itself, with its dictionary meaning of strict, frugal, laconic, characterized by self-denial. In this accounting, Sparta is engulfed by Stoicism. But Sparta was anything but Stoic. Instead, Sparta was a lyric, sportive state where courage flourished together with all the rituals of manhood, but not at the expense of sensual camaraderie saturated with Eros. The Spartan color was red; the scarlet cape the emblem of her warriors. Spartan courage was legendary, but so too was her system of education, which may have prospered because it maintained a connection to the most archaic traditions of the warrior band, while also nourishing them with the embryonic spirit of a cosmopolitan culture. The wisdom of Sparta preserved the mystery of the men's lodge in the syssitia where the elders of this tribal state ate, drank and slept together after having shared as boys the ordeals and wilderness of masculine initiation. Spartan music and lyricism also won the admiration of her countrymen who regularly journeyed there to participate in festivals. The liberty and sensuality of Spartan women were the scandal of the rest of Greece. For Spartans, the sexes coexisted within a field of paradox rather than polarity; that is to say, in Sparta, each sex fulfilled its nature, with masculinity becoming more masculine and femininity becoming more feminine without the need for transcendence into an androgynous ideal.

As Thucydides observed, Sparta was a state built upon the image of a secret society. Sparta was a state erected upon the ethos we have been advancing. Sparta was the flower and type, the historical perfection, of a community founded upon courage.

The time has come, it seems to me, to ennoble the idea, and ideally, even the experience of AIDS by following Adler's master, Nietzsche, who writes in a note beneath a heading called, "The Ennobling of Reality" about how the Greek imagination transformed disease. He writes:

> Because men once took the aphrodisiacal drive to be a godhead, showing worshipful gratitude when they felt its effect, that emotion has in the courage of time been permeated with higher kinds of ideas, and thus in fact greatly ennobled. By virtue of this idealizing art, some peoples have turned diseases into great beneficial forces of culture — the Greeks, for example, who in earlier

centuries suffered from widespread nervous epidemics (similar to epilepsy and the St. Vitus Dance) and created the glorious prototype of the bacchante from them. For the health of the Greeks was not at all robust; their secret was to honor illness like a god, too, if only it were powerful.

I have striven to ennoble AIDS because, as Nietzsche hints, from ennoblement comes power — the power to wield the sword, chivalry, bushido, and to conscript time, toil and resource in the noble service of finding a successful treatment and prevention of this fatal disease.

Interview with Asa Baber
by Lyman Grant

For 10 years, Asa Baber has written the "Men" column for *Playboy* magazine. Born in Chicago at the end of the Depression, Asa went on to graduate from Princeton in 1958 and serve in the Marine Corps from 1958 to 1961. He has published a novel about the war in Laos, *The Land of a Million Elephants*, and a volume of short stories, *Tranquillity Base and Other Stories*. His *Playboy* columns are collected in *Naked at Gender Gap*, published in 1992. MAN! editor Lyman Grant interviewed Asa for the "Representative Man" feature in the Spring, 1992 issue.

MAN!: Asa, you are a man who knows what he believes and is willing to stand by those beliefs when — we might say especially when — those beliefs are unpopular. That seems to be an admirable quality whether one agrees with your views or not. Where did you learn to stand by your convictions?

Asa: Let me say first that when you call me a "Representative Man," that does not mean that I think that I speak for every man. And it is important for me to say that because I can be misperceived by some guys as thinking that I speak for others, for all of men. I am not. I am one man speaking about a representative male life, whatever that is. As to my instinct toward self-destruction and stubbornness, I guess I am a man who is willing to be politically incorrect when it is necessary. The first place I would go to describe where I got that is genetically. It is my family. My people are Illinois, Indiana, Kentucky farm people. I am the first male in my family to go to college. I think there exists in my family tradition that Scotch-Irish, mule-stubborn quality of country people who say, "You can push me just this far." The second place I would go, I guess, would be when I was 14 years old. I had been raised on Chicago's South Side on 42nd Street, which was a fairly tough neighborhood and a declining neighborhood. I had my leather jacket, my bad case of acne, greasy hair and bad dress. I got lifted out of there and sent to a very fancy prep school on the East Coast. I was certainly politically incorrect in the prep school, particularly at first. And as a 14-year-old kid I had to figure out how much of myself I gave up to please the more snobbish of the faculty and students who were there. And I made a decision to go only about half way. I think

147

it was at that point that I learned how prejudiced people can be, how unfair they can be, and how sometimes you have to stand up for who you are, no matter who you are. I would say that was one of the most difficult and formative experiences in my life.

MAN!: How were you chosen to be lifted from that circumstance?

Asa: It was a combination of things. My grandmother had some money and could help towards my tuition. I was a fairly good athlete. I was a fast little shit. At 14, I could run the 100-yard dash in 10.3 or something. So the combination of that and the knowledge that I was already deeply into trouble. I was a fighter, something of a kleptomaniac. I had already done drugs; I had already experimented sexually. By the age of 14, I was not exactly an innocent. There was this sense on my part and my family's part that if I didn't get out of there, I would end up in very deep shit.

MAN!: You say in one of your pieces that your father was a non-drinking alcoholic.

Asa: Yes, I said that he was an alcoholic who never took a drink while I was alive. My dad was an alcoholic; he was a man who drank very heavily when he was very young, particularly in high school and college. I guess he went to about one semester at the University of Illinois and then he dropped out. I believe that alcohol was one of the reasons. Also when my father came to Chicago, he had no money at all. He was 19 or 20 and got a job in the Stephen's Hotel, which in now the Conrad Hilton. It was then the world's largest hotel. He got a job in the mail room, sorting mail. When he was done sorting mail, he would take some mail bags and sleep on the shelves of the mail room and then go back to work. He was really broke and really in trouble. And I think as just a matter of will power, my dad decided he could not drink and survive. And he just quit. He was a very courageous man. A very embittered man in some ways, a very humorous man, but a lot of balls.

MAN!: But like most fathers at the time, he wasn't home much?

Asa: In terms of my relationship with my father, it was the old story of the father who is embittered, disappointed, angry and takes out a fair share of hostility on the son. He is distant from the son and then later regrets it.

MAN!: You've written in a piece about your mother that because of his distance your mother turned to you.

Asa: My mother and I had what was basically an Oedipal relationship. She was a great lady, a dear, dear lady, loving and supportive. But

148

let us just say that she loved me too much in some ways. Particularly in my younger years and, I think, made the mistake of almost placing me in the role of husband. Which is a lot of pressure on a kid. And a lot of guys will know what I am talking about. My mother was an orphan who was raised by an aunt and uncle in Gibson City, Illinois. She was just as literate and bright and humorous and beautiful as could be. But she also suffered greatly from a sense of no self-worth. I think she tried to gain self-worth through me, at least in my formative years.

MAN!: You wrote that that tie was broken when you left Chicago at the age of 14.

Asa: Well, I had to break it, but in some ways that tie is never broken. But I was conscious very much that I had to get away from my mother, that her love was too possessive and too overwhelming.

MAN!: I'm sure a lot of men identify with this. Many of us are conscious that we have to break away from one or both of our parents simply to grow up.

Asa: It's a matter of identity. Frankly, I believe that all the work we are doing in this field of men's work is about establishing a sense of identity, of individuality. And this age tries to take away identity real vigorously.

MAN!: How so?

Asa: That's a whole other subject. In this culture we are nothing but markets, potential spenders, potential consumers. So many many forces are trying to get our money, our vote. They try to influence and manipulate us. And by the time you get through the day, you wonder who the hell you are, as everybody is trying to get a piece of you. It is my thesis, anyway, that male identity is more tenuous, particularly at an early age, than a lot of people give it credit for being. We have to work real hard to know that we are men. I think that is what this work is about: saying that it is OK to be male and by the way now you can take a look at yourself and figure out why and how you're male and what it is to be male. And I think it is very strengthening work.

MAN!: In a recent article about you in the Chicago Tribune, *one of your colleagues says that your columns seem to have a defensive quality about them. "Asa's always bleeding," the colleague said. Another way of looking at it is that you've become a great defender, an apologist for men.*

Asa: There is truth in almost every criticism, isn't there? I am sure there are times when I've been too defensive. But given the history of the last 25 years, I don't think it is a great sin to defend masculinity. It is my view that masculinity is roundly trashed every day. I'll give you a quick example from today. A producer from a television talk show called me. She outlined a show they were doing later in the week. They are having a male feminist and a woman who has done research on male aggression, and basically they are going to talk about how awful and aggressive and terrible the male is. They wanted to know if I wanted to come on that show, and I told them that quite frankly I am very tired of ambushes and I don't have a great need to be there. The producer said, "Well, as you know, men are the standards by which we judge everything and men have all the power." How many times have I heard that? So I have defended masculinity, and have at times been too defensive. But what wasn't mentioned in the *Tribune* piece is that sometimes I just sit down and boogie and goof around. It's not all sincerity.

MAN!: Yet you do seem to love men, not as men might have been, in a romancing of some past of kings and warriors and magicians. And not a beautiful vision of what men might become. You love men as they are, right now, today.

Asa: Exactly right. Just regular guys.

MAN!: So what's so lovable about regular guys?

Asa: Well, basically, I think they anchor the world. As the feminists go off and trash masculinity, and as some of the mythopoetic guys go off and get in touch with their King, Warrior, Magician, Lover, and as everybody just floats off the earth into some stratosphere, the regular guys — the truckers, the farmers, the cops, the firemen, the newspaper vendors, the taxi drivers, and all the regular guys — they keep the humor going, they make the tough choices, they commit their lives to their families, they deal with the violence of the world. I think they are wonderful. I hope that in this men's work we can be much more inclusive, and always work with those guys. The smartest people in the world are everywhere. I've known some Marine Corps Gunnery Sergeants as smart, as well-read, and as shrewd as any college professor I ever met. We have to remember that regular guys are fine, thank you very much.

MAN!: But isn't it in some ways these regular guys who are the wife-beaters, the child abusers. . .

Asa: Let me stop you right there. You look at wife-beating and it goes across the economic scale. And you can find husband-beating, too. I think it is one of the most snobbish things in the world to suggest that because we have an economic clout or a college degree that it places some men above others.

MAN!: So let me ask, does men's work offer anything to the average guy?

Asa: What the average guy needs is support from other men — in particular, support for the idea that masculinity is a good quality. I feel that the average guy will never choose to deal with the more exotic rituals of much of the Bly work or with the Jungian vocabulary. But the average guy certainly feels ambushed and trapped by feminist rhetoric, by pressures to perform as a breadwinner, a good mate, a good father. Just an awful lot of unpublished great men think about all the issues that we talk about. They don't necessarily talk about them, but they sure as hell think about them. One of the deepest and most unfair criticisms of men is the whole idea that since men don't talk as much as women or verbalize as rapidly that they're poor communicators.

MAN!: As a young man, you served in the Marine Corps. What did that experience teach you about the nature of men?

Asa: Well, first of all, I happen to think that the Marine Corps is one of the finest organizations in the world. I believe that my experience in the Marines was a very grounding experience. I use that almost jokingly, too. We covered a lot of ground, and we dug a lot of earth. What the Marine Corps did for me was take me out of the precious Ivy League environment and put me back on the street where I belong. There are traditions and loyalties in the Marines that are incredible. The care and the training that, for example, my drill instructors gave me was just outstanding.

MAN!: The first Men column that you wrote, in April, 1982, was titled "Role Models" and there you wrote about your drill instructor, Danny Gross.

Asa: I owe my life to him. During that boot camp, he became a very good friend and a real role model for me. If you want to know a group of just great men, go down and meet a bunch of drill instructors in a Marine boot camp. You will laugh your ass off. They are they funniest human beings on earth; they are the toughest, and they are the most demanding. They give of themselves — I mean, just the physical energy it takes to be a drill instructor. They are just great men. And you learn in the Marine Corps how to take care of your own. If you're in charge of some men, you have to make sure they don't have trench foot; you have to make sure that they are well fed; you've got to make sure that if you are in an ambush you can get them all out; that you just don't suddenly leave somebody behind because you forgot them. There is a sense of loyalty. The Marine is just the essence of the stand-up guy.

MAN!: It seems that your drill instructor served as a mentor. And you wrote that soon or later, younger men turn to you as a role model. What does it mean to be a mentor?

Asa: I'll put it this way: I think we are very simple and primitive creatures. As men, almost everything we learn is by imitation. How did you learn to hit a baseball? You watch guys hit baseballs. We imitate each other physically and how we treat one another. I think that this is the essence of male initiation. Men teach other men how to behave. That's what mentoring is. I think another name for it is brothering. Fathering, sometimes. I think it is much more often like the older brother saying, here's how you hold the curve ball. To some degree, I think it is how we show our love for one another. We don't talk a lot about it. We just say, "Here, let me show you how I build this back porch." That's how we communicate.

MAN!: When Robert Bly was in Austin in 1989, he tossed out the comment that a father's role might just be to express conditional love. Fathers are critical; fathers are judgmental. Perhaps it is the mentor, the older brother, that expresses the unconditional love for other men. Perhaps we need both kinds of love.

Asa: We do need both. But I think that as fathers we need to learn to be more unconditional in our love. I would like to think that as a father, I was basically unconditional in my love for my sons. I am sure that I was also critical of my sons. But I hope at heart, they understood and understand that I'm going to love them, no matter what. But you've raised an interesting point, because there is a way that when men deal with other men we set up certain boundaries, certain standards. We do show our displeasure if those standards are crossed.

MAN!: The drill sergeant has to do that to protect the whole company.

Asa: You bet. And one of the great things about drill sergeants is that they do so with humor. It is not politically correct humor, but it's humor. I can remember my first 36 hours down in Quantico, when you are basically in shock, and this guy was chewing gum, and this drill instructor comes up to him and says, "What are you chewing, maggot face? Foreskin?" And I just cracked up.

MAN!: You mentioned initiation. It is widely held that boys are not initiated into manhood and that they greatly need that.

Asa: Men need to be initiated. Honest to God. It is not an age thing anymore. There are a lot of men who don't know they are men.

MAN!: How come they don't and what will it take to initiate them so they know they are men?

Asa: We live in a very emasculating culture, OK? First of all, we have had this very necessary cultural revolution, the feminist revolution. It had to happen and it is very important that it did happen. But it also has its excesses and one of its favorite excesses is that for about 25 years men have been told that they are evil, oppressors, they don't get it, and on and on. Then the IRS emasculates us: "Here I will tell you how much money I made. Please tell me me how much I can keep." Corporate culture emasculates us. Everybody has to be hypocritical and smile when they don't mean it. I just think that men are placed under enormous pressures to establish an identity.

MAN!: You have been involved with the New Warrior Training Adventure, which is exploring the process of men initiating men. And you wrote about your involvement in a recent article, "The Call of the Wild." What attracted you to their work?

Asa: The New Warriors were the first group of men that I had found that were not just mythopoetic and weren't just feminists. They had their own original stamp. And it was a wonderful, vigorous, humorous, demanding stamp on the whole process of male initiation. I can't tell you how much I loved that weekend.

MAN!: What happened that weekend to make it so powerful?

Asa: The first thing to say is that it is a very creative and demanding process. The New Warrior Training Adventure is the title of the first of many weekends that they have constructed and devised. As you know, it is all confidential, so I am not going to sit here and describe what happens on a weekend, even though you can go to other places and find it described. I signed a pledge of confidentiality that I will not break . . . .

MAN!: There's one of the beauties of men — the ability to say that "I can hold that secret."

Asa: Absolutely! I think it is very unmanly to sign a pledge that says I will not reveal what goes on during this weekend and go out and chatter about it. But I can say what happened to me during my weekend. Two wonderful men led me through a process whereby I first got in touch with my survivors' guilt. As a man I have seen far too many of my brothers and friends disappear or die or be killed. They helped me deal with that enormous burden that was holding me back and that was haunting me so much and I finally focused down on a Marine buddy of mine who died in a helicopter crash and for whom I have mourned all of my life and felt that I should have died, not him, and all the stuff that guys feel. I managed with the help of these two men to really confront that and deal with it for the first time. I don't say I completely put it behind me, but I looked at that shadow and I confronted it.

MAN!: Many people dislike the magazine you write for. Would you care to defend Playboy?

Asa: I really hope that the men's movement will become less puritanical and judgmental about this magazine. If *Playboy* did not exist, I would never have been published over the last 25 years. It was the only place that had the courage to publish my politically incorrect work and that goes back to the novel I wrote about the war in Laos, which *Playboy* serialized in 1970. *Playboy* stood against that war. Also, I believe *Playboy* has stood for men. I know that a number of folks in the men's movement are offended by the magazine, and in all honesty, I don't understand it. The last time I checked I did not mind looking at beautiful naked women, and it did not turn me into a rapist. The masculinity that I possess is, among other things, very sexual, very bawdy. I love sexual fantasy. As I say in one of my columns, I think that the fact that you can buy any number of romance novels at most Seven-Elevens today, but you may not be able to find a copy of *Playboy* says basically that female fantasy in this culture is OK and that male fantasy is not. I've seen the magazine burned; I've seen it shredded; I've seen pickets stand in front of bookstores and protest it; I've seen people like Robert Bly be very condescending about it and talk about how tired he is of *Playboy* and how tired he is of men being boys. I think through it all, *Playboy* has been loyal to men. Frankly, and I guess this will anger many people, I think that the part of the men's movement that tries to suggest that our sexuality has to be more pure and less lustful really betrays men. It betrays men to suggest that we should be ashamed of our sexuality.

MAN!: Does it betray women?

Asa: Yep. I do believe there are literally millions of women out there who are waiting for men just to be men. Come on, you guys are sexual; admit it. Come on, you guys, stop apologizing for who you are. Stop being ashamed for who you are.

MAN!: Another criticism of Playboy *is that it encourages and feeds the addictions of our culture. How would you respond?*

Asa: If we are talking about sex addiction, I don't know where to go with that unless we define it more thoroughly. I don't think that sexual fantasy is sexual addiction. I am not suggesting that sexual addiction doesn't exist, but I honestly believe that for 99 percent of the men who read *Playboy* that it does not stimulate them to go out and be sex addicts. In terms of liquor ads and cigarette ads, I can only say that I live in the real

154

world. I do not touch liquor at all, and at one time I drank like a fish. I consider myself very much into recovery from alcoholism. I know that alcohol damaged my body a lot and my mind. At the same time, I don't think advertising is the problem. My sense of my own alcoholism is that I drank to hide the pain of my survivor's guilt. I literally was ashamed I was alive. I literally wanted to be dead, because so many good men I knew, including men I grew up with on the south side of Chicago, had disappeared, died, or been killed. I didn't deal well with that. So it wasn't a liquor ad that got or kept me drinking. It was a deep, deep personal pain. When I say I live in the real world, what I mean is that in today's market a magazine that rejects liquor ads and cigarette ads and other ads that offend certain groups would have a very difficult time reaching 14 million readers. So I do not agree with those who say that the magazine enhances addictions.

MAN!: In many ways, you lived the great American intellectual's life. You had a tenured position teaching English at the University of Hawaii. And you resigned. Why did you do such a stupid thing?

Asa: Well, I've never been very bright. The first reason is a purely personal one. I had lost custody of my two sons in a very bitter divorce. I did not trust my ex-wife's ability to raise them. She was taking them back to the mainland, and I felt a great need to be near them geographically. But I also left Hawaii because it was too easy. If I had remained a tenured professor, I would have had a lifetime job, but I would not necessarily have been very challenged by that. The experience in Hawaii was probably a little narrow for me; if I were going to be a writer, I would have to live a life of some risks and not from within the safety of the academic world. Finally, I was fairly popular with the students and a good teacher by my standards, but quite a few of my colleagues did not necessarily respect me nor enjoy my company, and I didn't feel it was a collegial atmosphere in some ways. I still have good friends there, but I am not an academic man.

MAN!: How well then did your relationship with your sons go?

Asa: That is one of the great triumphs of my life. I am a father who has two sons in their 20s now, and they are still talking me. They even return my phone calls. I think that is a miracle. We have stayed loyal to one another, the three of us, through hell and high water. There were many years when they were very young when a number of people tried to tell them terrible things about me and tried to keep us from seeing each other, and through it all they just maintained a love for me and I for them. And nobody could tear us apart.

The Love of a Mentor
by Lyman Grant

I will plant companionship thick as trees along the rivers of America,
and along the shores of the Great Lakes, and all over the
prairies.
I will make inseparable cities with their arms about each other's
necks,
By the love of comrades,
By the manly love of comrades.

— Walt Whitman

My friendship with William A. Owens, the man who was willing to be my mentor, began 13 years before I met him. One spring night in 1963, my mother again lost her temper and began whipping me with a leather belt. I was only 10 years old, but I knew that this night her whipping would stop. I yanked the belt from her, and she never tried to whip me again.

My friendship with Bill deepened six years later. My mother had been dead for a year. In a blizzard of mutual hatred, my father and I fought over her memory and what she meant to us. I threw him against the kitchen wall, held him by the collar, and for the first time in my life saw fear in his eyes.

By the time I entered the University of Texas, I knew that I had failed both of my parents. I was Lyman Winstead Grant, Jr., and quite aware of what I should accomplish. I should major in business management and become a personnel director like my father; I should join the ROTC, and my father, a retired Lieutenant Colonel, could proudly pin his own Lieutenant's bars upon my shoulders. It was 1971 and I would do none of these things.

By the time I met Bill Owens in 1976, I was a lost young man with fear in my eyes and a hole in my chest. From the time I was a junior in high school, I had been emotionally on my own. Without knowing it, I had no parents. Because I was independent, rebellious, contemptuous, diffident, secretive of my talents, I attracted no adults who looked out for me, cared for me, listened to me, taught me. I desperately needed an older man, a man with authority, to tell me that what I felt was understandable, that what I desired was good and possible, that what I had done in my family relationships was acceptable.

All I knew was what I had read in Shakespeare, Thoreau and Plato, on the one hand, and Hemingway and Fitzgerald on the other. I identified with the wounded men the latter wrote about, but hoped against hope that I could find the wisdom of the former. God, I was lost. I could see lights in the distance, but saw no path at my feet. If I believed my father, I would never find it. In one of our many arguments, my father shouted that I would never be a writer because it was not in my genes to be one.

Then I met Bill Owens, and my life changed. I was 22 and had enrolled in graduate school in English without my father's knowledge. Bill was 70 years old and recently retired as dean and professor emeritus from Columbia University. Having just published his 11th book, he was returning to Texas A&M as its writer-in-residence, where he had begun his college teaching career 30 years earlier, to begin writing his 12th book. When he arrived, I did not know the range of his work or the awards he had won. Nor did I know that he had been born in a family of poor dirt farmers in Northeast Texas, that his father died the day Bill was born, that he had struggled against all odds to get an education and become a writer.

I knew only that in the 1940s and '50s he had been the protegé of Roy Bedichek, the author of one of my favorite books, *Adventures With a Texas Naturalist*. When I volunteered to be Bill's graduate assistant, I thought that I might learn something about Texas and nature; I never dreamed I was meeting a man who had overcome almost every obstacle life presented him, who was dedicated to teaching other young men to do the same. I did not know that I was meeting the man who would initiate me into manhood.

Now that I have become involved with the men's movement, I understand what I experienced. As men like Robert Bly have explained, a boy must go through several stages to become a man, stages our society does not make clear. Growing up, a young boy will bond with and separate from his mother, then bond with and separate from his father. As the man begins his career, if he is lucky, he will find or be found by a mentor, what Bly calls "the male-mother."

I prefer the term "male-mother." The word "mentor" connotes a purely professional relationship between master and apprentice. The mentor in the usual sense is someone in a position of authority, such as the vice-president in a business or a professor in a university, who takes an interest in the work of younger colleagues. Mentors will discuss with the young protegés problems of a strictly professional nature; sometimes, mentors will serve as conduits to information or to other influential professionals. The male-mother performs all these, but he also nurtures the young man, cares for his entire being, his intellect and his soul.

One of the first lessons Bill Owens taught me was that success need not be bought by bartering joy. I had committed myself to write a tedious and meaningless thesis, but being the son of a personnel director, I thought success lay in boredom. Through Bill's example and his candid conversations, I learned the difference between the academic mind and the creative mind. I knew which I wanted to develop in myself and in my students. I knew which Bill believed I had a talent for. A few months later, when I read J. Frank Dobie's statement about dissertations' being the transference of bones from one grave to another, I understood. I wrote the chairman of the department, asking to change thesis advisors and topics.

The lessons have continued as Bill tries to move me beyond thinking like a writer to loving like a man. In a conversation last year, we talked about the teacher's responsibilities to the whole student, not just to his or her intellect. He told me of a time 40 years ago when a student appeared at his house. "I've come to tell you I'm killing myself," the student told him. "I had to drop everything. I had to stay with him and talk, no matter how long," Bill told me. Bill's crystalline eyes told me more. Although Bill was 83, retired for more than a dozen years, at that moment he was face-to-face with that desperate student. He had never stopped loving him, caring for his development. Their talk had helped. The student graduated and led a happy, successful life.

Bill Owens' ability and willingness to help young men (and he has helped dozens) is one of the wonders of this world, an example of how Nature compensates for loss. Orphaned by his father's death, he grew up in a strong matriarchy. From this early experience, Bill discovered the importance of older men in the lives of younger men. Throughout his life, he searched for and found several men who recognized in him his own good heart and curious mind.

In his book, *Three Friends*, Bill writes of a time when he turned to Bedichek, not for professional advice, but for nurturing, care, understanding. During the Depression, Bill traveled to the prison at Sugar Land to collect black folk songs. Instead of finding song, Bill discovered institutionalized racism. He drove straight to Austin, awoke Bedichek, and talked with him long into the night. "I had never heard anyone so sympathetic to the Negro, or so concerned over the Negro question," Bill writes. "He helped me understand a lesson I had begun to learn that day: to a collector, people must be more important than their folklore." This was a lesson that would eventually lead Owens to become a writer instead of a folklorist.

As a writer, Bill has devoted much attention to the rites of passage necessary to become a man, the development of a strong sense of character, of values and integrity. His third novel, *Look to the River*, about a young country boy in the 1920s, is a direct exploration of the mentor-protegé relationship. Although his character, young Jed, has found surrogate parents who will care for him, he has no chance to grow to his potential until he meets traveling John. Because of his fear and his innocence, Jed makes mistakes that, without John's aid, would have hurt him greatly. Toward the end of the novel, Jed asks, "How come you done this for me, John?" John replies, almost as Bill might reply to my same question, "It ain't easy, being a boy like you, so somebody's got to help — somebody that's been through it. I'm old now, but a long way back I went through it — not the same, but close enough." In one of my copies of *Look to the River*, Bill has written, "To Lyman Grant, a Jed of sorts."

The influence of a male-mother is broad and deep; the most important ways are personal, not professional. Although I was deeply honored when he asked me to be the co-editor of the volume of letters by Roy Bedichek, his mentor, I hold just as dear the smaller kindnesses Bill showed me. He talked with me about women and sex. He recited poetry with me. He told me of times when he was frightened and hopeless about his writing. He gave me his volume of Walt Whitman's poetry and wrote inside, "I am now giving you this book because I want you to love it." We walked through fields of wildflowers, and he told me what Bedichek had to say about them. He complimented me by soliciting my opinion on his works in progress. Most important, he listened to me talk endlessly, pointlessly, until I had found myself.

In finding myself, I let go of my father. I was given a choice of what kind of man I wanted to be. Over the years, Bill and I had often discussed his experiences in World War II. Since his experiences and opinions were so dramatically different from my father's, I listened carefully. When my father was drafted, he was offended and outraged. He viewed being a private as a personal insult and struggled single-mindedly to become an officer. He was proud he spent the entire war behind a desk in Nashville, Tennessee. Bill, on the other hand, volunteered and served most of the war as a sergeant, much of it in the Pacific Theater. My father and Bill even admired different generals. My father greatly admired Douglas MacArthur, while Owens praised Walter Krueger as the common soldier's general. Bill's latest book, *Eye-Deep in Hell*, about his experiences in World War II, is often critical of MacArthur's pomposity.

The contrast between the two men — my father and my mentor — became primarily a contrast in values. One man was elitist, the other democratic; one selfish, the other dutiful; one timid and safe, the other brave and adventurous. I knew whose values I admired and could follow.

My friendship with Bill Owens, therefore, meant that one day I would recognize that by the age of 17 I had overcome the hold my parents had on me. My will to know myself was stronger than theirs to confine me. It has taken me 20 years to understand and accept it.

A small, but personally significant act finally cut the chains. Fully aware of the importance of his suggestion, when it came time to type the title page of the book we edited together, Bill suggested that I drop the Jr. after my name. In this seemingly trivial act, I claimed a name and an identity that had always been denied me. I was no longer Lyman Jr., pale reflection of my father. Instead, I stole my father's name from him. I did not know who this new Lyman Grant was, but whoever he was, I was he, and despite his raising, he had his name on a book.

In one of the Calamus poems Bill and I read together, Whitman writes "Your novitiate would even then be long and exhausting, / The whole past theory of your life and all conformity to the lives around you would have to be abandon'd." So it was with me. Although my father and I began to accept each other and understand each other's differences — I was at his side when he died two years ago — we finally released each other to live our separate lives.

My father and I seldom spoke about my writing; only once did we speak about Bill Owens. I began talking about the process of getting books published and how grateful I was to Bill for asking me to work with him, and how much I learned from him because he included me in all stages of publication. I talked too much, and the next thing I noticed was that my 75-year-old father had stepped into the adjoining room, slacked-shouldered, head bent. Unmistakably, he was crying and hiding his tears from me. I said no more, then or the few remaining years that my father lived.

At that moment, my father realized he had lost me. Little did he know that he had lost me years before, when he decided that since I would not emulate him, he would not encourage me in anything else. It troubles me that my father would cry about the love another man gave me. I did not want to hurt him. But if it took my father's tears for me to know Bill and appreciate what he has given to me, I would make my father cry and cry again.

Soul Fatigue

(Anonymous)

I have grown weary of the game. There seems to be no point to it at all. The narrow, "get ahead" American dream, as played out in corporations, is nothing but a big, fat lie. I am gut sick of being conned. I am fatigued of the lies. All kinds of wonderful promises are made, but none are carried out. Work hard, be creative, achieve, acquire degrees, and the good life will be yours. Well, these are false promises. The only criteria that holds in American corporate life now is sickeningly simple. You are measured only in relationship to how you affect quarterly profits. All other criteria are insignificant. The greed and ruthless ambition of financial game players has reduced the public life and corporate culture to a short-term, cutthroat fight for survival. Meanwhile, our country is bashed by foreign competition, where cooperation and long-range commitment to a public good is held much higher than the ruthless greed of financial people.

Housing is also a real problem (as breadwinner for a family of four, I speak from experience). It is senseless and stupid to pay $500 to $1200 per month for 30 years to have decent shelter. This is outrageous! This is bondage of the worst kind. The American dream, as pushed by the federal government, banks, and rich developers in collaboration with local zoning authorities, keeps middle-class people in a horrible, grinding debt most of their adult lives. Now, the fact that kids are growing up on drugs, totally out of balance, is not surprising, considering how much abuse their parents endure every day.

The economic machine that our culture has become requires that people be driven by compulsive desire to have more and more and more. More of everything must be acquired, so that we can feed the gnawing, empty void in the pit of our being. We feel hollow at the core. The greater our sense of alienation, the fiercer and more intense is our compulsive behavior. We are consumed by our consumption.

My sense of futility is both pervasive and profound. I am surrounded by humanity, and yet I am completely alone.

Crowded to the point of suffocation, yet isolated.

Separate, dying of thirst in a sea of soulless selves.

Connected by all the chains of external bondage, yet the feelings are savagely severed from my soul.

I have recently watched a show on PBS called *Bradshaw on the Family*. He talks about compulsion as a way of controlling feelings. God! I am seeing compulsions everywhere I look. In myself, in my wife, in the people at work. Commercial TV is a never-ending stream of audiovisual, compulsive clamor. The stuff that insanity is made of. Our culture is primarily a web of interlocking, compulsive connectivity. Now, there is a real oxymoron — "compulsive connectivity." To be driven compulsively is to be fundamentally severed from the ground of being. And yet, in an unbelievably paradoxical sense, we in our culture are joined in a common grip of compulsion. We all share a sense of being driven. The state of being compulsive is our state of being. Compulsion is the tide that binds us. So we are related to one another, and yet we are not related at all. It is as if we are automatons being controlled by remote control. What we share is our unrelatedness.

I remember coming to the realization that I was not going to find peace with "the right job." I started to realize that I had problems that were manifested in many situations in my past. I felt a sense of desperate terror. What was I going to do now? Now that I realized that no magic, external situation will save me? My God, what a feeling of despair.

For the last eight years, I have been in a compulsive quest to be on the cutting edge of software technology. I believed that being on the cutting edge would "fix my life." I would have the good life. I would have creative freedom, wealth, professional prestige and power. I would have a sense of personal contentment. Well, I have made a lot of money and lost it all when real-estate prices went crash. I have authored a patent on a product of great commercial success. I have written and published a paper in a classy, professional, technical journal. I have worked for some of the most prestigious companies in America. I have earned two BS degrees and an MS in Computer Science with a 4.0 grade-point average. In short, I have achieved many great successes. Yet through it all, my internal feeling has been one of being not quite good enough. My personal feeling of inadequacy has never been changed by any of these successes. Also, the promises held out for achieving have never really been kept. I have been paid more for being technically competent. But increased pay has been the only real pay-off. The power in hierarchical organizations is only available to those who become shrewd in the matters of politics, money and power. Scientific, technical and creative talent are all second-class skills in the dominant corporate culture. The most mediocre manager makes more than the most brilliant engineer. They are two separate classes.

Now, in my deep state of burn-out, I am really confused. I feel my energy is blocked. I am afraid of committing myself to much of anything. I am perhaps compulsively afraid of being compulsively consumed again, yet hanging back seems so lifeless. I am in my own personal purgatory.

I am afraid that I may snap. I am afraid that my cell of motivation has dried up. I am caught in a dangerous dilemma. I feel I should support my family, and yet I feel a need to break away from working as a technical person in corporate America. If I totally leave behind my technical skills, my family and I will be reduced to near-starvation wages. To maintain a middle-class way of life, I must continue in my narrow, professional role. The only escape from this dilemma seems to be to greatly reduce costs and get my wife involved in bringing home some revenue. Neither of these tactics seem likely to happen for a long time. It may take two to five years. Meanwhile, I have many days when I have trouble getting out of bed and going through the motions of "being a professional." This trap is sheer hell.

The Great Hunt

by Bill Jeffers

Sitting in the shade on the front porch
I saw
a streak moving through the air above the grass.
A dark missile.
A sparrow.
And in the glare I saw, shining,
trailing two feet behind the tiny bird,
the glint of something green
like ribbon,
possibly like grass.
Something for its nest.
It flew to the eaves of the house next door,
deposited the prize
and leapt into thin air
for another.

Inside the Handy Dan the aisles are swarming with guys.
Lots of guys are here. We are all here
getting stuff for our houses.
Everyone is walking around searching for the things they want
because there is no help at Handy Dan,
there are no helpers and there are no hints,
there are only people to take your money at the end.
So, everyone is walking around in-search-of.
It is the Great Hunt.

All the guys are hunting in the aisles of Handy Dan.
We are walking past each other and getting in each other's way.
Mostly we do not acknowledge each other.
We do not push shopping carts.
We walk with our big arms swinging and our big dicks tucked inside
      our pants.

It is quiet.
This is not a social place.
It is a hunting ground.
We are intent.
Most of us would say we are on an errand,
but it is something deeper than that,
something older.
We are the Men, and this
is the Great Hunt.

I don't like some of the guys as I pass them.
They look weird. They're dressed funny.
Some of them look absolutely stupid
wandering around like that.
This happens before an explanation can take shape.
Instantly. Automatically. I just don't like them.
I feel
like an animal.
I imagine the hair on the back of my neck
standing straight up as we walk past each other,
whether I want it to or not. Some of these are really big guys.
My flag.
Watch out! Get away! Back off!
I could find myself behind my rage mask:
   face contorted, teeth bared, growling
   The low sound would leap out on its own, menacing and lethal.
   I would be frightened by it, too.

Lots of guys are here inside the Handy Dan. We are all here.
Everyone is walking around in-search-of.
It is the Great Hunt.

We are wearing our work clothes.
Many of us have already been outside in the sun.
We are hot and we have a smell.
We are in a hurry and we don't know where anything is
and we have a lot of work to do when we get back home.

Now, I have finally found the place I need to be
and I am looking for just the right size hex head bolt
to permanently repair the hasp on my fence.
I am getting close, I can feel it,
The hunter senses the quarry nearby.
I am aware of the hex head bolts trying to be invisible,
or trying to hide by looking like lag bolts or screws;
but this is very personal now; I can almost smell the one I want.
I am getting closer and closer. . .
when another guy comes up and starts looking in the bins right beside
me.
He is odd.
There is something definitely wrong with him. Definitely.
A bit retarded if you want to know the truth.
He is not quite all there.
Look at the way he's fumbling around in there.
Hey! That's the bolt I was looking for!

I have completely stopped looking for my hex-head bolt.
I frown a little. Furrow my brows. Tooth Gleams.
I peer a bit more intently at the rack.
Shift the idea
of my weight toward the intruder,
without moving my body in the least.
His nostrils flare. He feels me get closer even though I haven't moved.
He is crowded in all of a sudden.
I feel the hair on the back of his neck begin to rise.
I feel the hair on the back of my neck begin to rise.
There is blood in the air. He is threatened.
He shifts his weight away. He becomes lighter on his toes.
I cough.
He takes one step.
I follow. One step.
I am not crowding him.
I'm just not allowing him to make any more room.
       I was here first.
I reach into a bin of bolts and scramble them around with my hand.
He jumps. I hesitate, and send my thought

to the bin directly in front of him.
He makes a break for it.
I can almost see his tail between his legs.

I want to pound my chest. This is my turf!
It feels right to be here once again.
I have room again. I can breathe again.
Now I can find what I was looking for.
That other guy's just going to have to wait, that's all.
This is my turf!
I almost unzip my pants
and pee all over the counter.

Lots of guys are here inside the Handy Dan. We are all here.
Everyone is walking around in-search-of.
It is the Great Hunt.
We are the Men.
Getting stuff
for our houses.

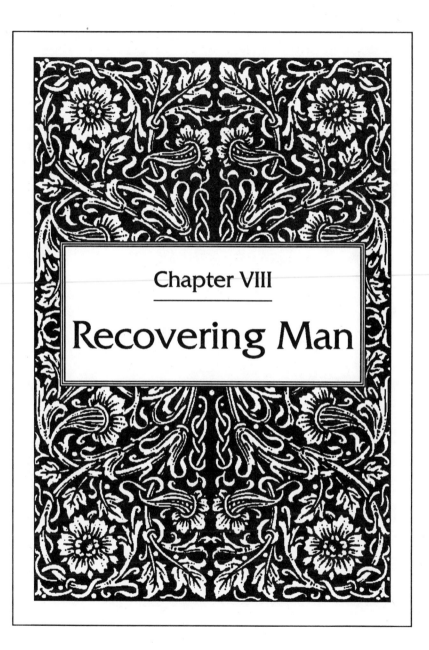

Chapter VIII

Recovering Man

Little Boy Lost:
A Man's Recovery from Sexual Abuse
by Ron Phillips

The windshield wipers squeaked a steady rhythm as November droplets kept disappearing before my eyes. I didn't look at the wipers, but I knew they were there. I sat numb and in shock, staring through the glass into the cold, rainy morning, looking for answers.

I finally got the courage to turn my head and look at the weeds fly by along the roadside and wondered if I could survive the fall should I jump from the speeding car. Why was this happening to me? What was I supposed to do? Could the oncoming cars see what this man was doing to me? Could they see his hand inside my pants?

I could see my reflection in the window. I focused on my baseball cap. I was too ashamed to look at my face. My world was ending. I would never be the same. I was an All-Star Little League player and dreamed of playing for the Yankees. I had dreamed earlier that morning of catching a big fish with the man in the car. He was a "friend of the family." But now those dreams fell away as the little boy I saw in the glass disappeared just like the raindrops.

Because I was a victim of sex abuse by a man, I would lose touch with that little boy. I almost never found him again. For more than 30 years, I was to struggle with the horror of living my life detached from myself emotionally. I spent more energy trying to look, act and feel normal and masculine than I did living life itself. I feared that someone somewhere would know and expose this dreaded, deep, dark secret and my life would truly be over.

I constantly guarded this secret. I almost died of shame, believing that I was bad and evil for what had happened. Because this man abused me several times, I thought I was to blame. I didn't realize until recently that I was the victim, not the cause of the problem.

It has been almost eight years since I entered therapy. My marriage was plagued with emotional abuse, infidelity and alcoholism. It was the therapy that led me to the Twelve-Step programs I now follow. At first, I thought the problems were all my fault and stemmed from the fact that I was defective in some way, incapable of coping or being happy.

171

The twisted and distorted thinking, as well as the outrageous behavior, was only a symptom of my buried pain. I was afraid to look at it at first, but the Twelve-Step programs suggest "admitting the exact nature of all my wrongs." I thought I was admitting my personal defects when actually I was letting the light shine on this dark and painful secret. I had to be told that I had been victimized before I believed that most of my life's problems were the result of the abuse. I had been trapped in the role of victim and saw myself as doomed to unhappiness and failure.

Victims of abuse need affirmation and validation from others. Adult men abused as children by men have not been able to receive help because of the fear of being outcast and labeled homosexual. Thanks to some safe and loving people, I have been able to bring my reality back into focus.

It has not been easy and it is not over. I still have pain and sadness over what happened when I was 12 years old. Since the first day of the abuse by the trusted family friend, I felt strange, weird, awful, dirty and isolated. But today is different. I am no longer overwhelmed by this problem. I am more than just OK. I feel excited and alive with my life. Occasionally the negative feelings return, but I now know where they come from and what to do about them.

I also know today that I am not alone. There are thousands of men who have suffered this same type of abuse. It just has never been safe to talk about it until now. Here are some truths that have changed my life:

1. The sensual pleasure experienced as a result of the abuse was normal.

I had been confused because the experience felt sensually stimulating. I felt overwhelming shame that I had secretly "enjoyed" the abuse and wasted great energy hiding that enjoyment. I had been afraid to think about it, much less admit to anyone that it felt good. I never realized the human body is made to enjoy stimulation in order to procreate. Infant boys whose genitals are stimulated will get erections.

It's natural. That is the way we are made. It did not mean I was defective. It meant I was normal!

2. The victim always feels like it is his fault.

A curious and confusing dynamic of abuse is that the victim believes, at some level, that he caused the abuse; that something inherent in him created the avenue for the abuser. Oddly enough, the abuser may feel like the victim and act accordingly when confronted. This was certainly true in my case. I felt guilty for not stopping the abuse. The truth is that I was a child and couldn't defend myself against the adult male.

3. I was set up to be afraid of women and distrustful of men.

Because my father was addicted to his work, he spent little time with me when I was growing up. I longed for his attention and approval and became vulnerable to men who might give me attention. I needed a hero. It is logical that I was so trusting of the man who took me fishing.

After the abuse I could no longer trust men, especially gay men. I desperately needed love and affirmation from older men, but feared trying to get it. My father is an ex-prizefighter. He is a quiet man who never lost his temper, but there was a sleeping volcano inside him. I couldn't do anything to upset him. I was in fear for my life from both my father and the abuser. I was trapped in the abuse. There was no way out. To make matters worse, I thought if I were a "real man," I would have stopped the abuse myself.

Likewise, my relationship with my mother was interrupted as a result of the abuse. It just wasn't safe to tell her what was going on. Fearing I would disappoint her, I guarded myself. The shame enclosed me in an emotional cage that cut me off from healthy interaction with women. I would not allow them to get close enough to feel their love. They might get too close to the secret. I had nowhere to turn. Submitting to the abuse seemed to be the only way out.

I was angry at my mother for a long time. I couldn't figure out how she could let this thing happen to me. Couldn't she tell I was hurting? I would not trust women with my intimate secrets and never thought they found me attractive. This was a major factor in my inability to be happy in my marriage. My wife wanted closeness that I was unable to provide.

Recently, my mother agreed to go to counseling with me to deal with this issue. She was unaware of the abuse, but remembers a change in my behavior. In particular, I lost my spontaneity. I used to dance in front of the television set to entertain the family. When I stopped the dancing, she didn't know what to do and assumed this was a stage I was going through.

4. I can take care of myself.

I never again felt safe after the abuse. Someone older and bigger had violated my boundary and shattered my spirit. I felt small and vulnerable to the world. Feeling like I was unable to protect myself, I constantly sought strong allies and relationships to protect me. I wasn't inadequate, I just felt that way. Actually, I went on to play baseball in high school and college. I had a family and by many standards was a success in the business community. I even owned my own business. Inside, though, I knew I didn't measure up. I needed someone to protect me. I didn't believe I had everything it takes to take care of myself.

Today, I know differently. Today, I know there was never anything wrong with me. I have learned that my healing has followed a natural course through the processes of de-shaming, reclaiming, committing and discovering.

Through the process called Shame Reduction, I have been able to break out of the death grip of what John Bradshaw calls "toxic shame." I now hold the abuser accountable for his shameless behavior. Without the burden of feeling bad about what had happened, my outlook and self-image gradually changed. I became aware of the concept of the inner child and began to nurture him. I soon knew I had been reunited with a part of me that had been missing for a long time. I had reclaimed that lost little boy who had been left in the rain, watching the windshield wipers.

I made a commitment to this inner child that I would never abandon him again and would always take care of him. I slowly began to trust myself to do just that. Once I made the commitment to stay with ME and help ME, my journey became more exciting. It has been painful, but always rewarding and always leading to joy and fulfillment.

I know I am not guilty and that I can overcome the fear and distrust. I know today I am adequate. There will be even more discovery if I am willing to go through the steps to uncover it. I no longer dread the work. I welcome it.

It is interesting to note that I have begun trusting my intuition, which has proven infallible in sensing the presence of abusers. When my little boy inside feels scared, I protect him.

I have forgiven my mother and father, and have begun a long overdue, healthy relationship with them. I am returning to wholeness and have known joy and bliss for the first time — two feelings I had known nothing about.

Today I know I am alive. There is no doubt about what I want in life. I have changed careers and love what I am doing. I am capable of feeling all my feelings and am often capable of giving unconditional love. I have reclaimed my heterosexuality and no longer fear women or men, whether they be gay or straight.

I am a real man today. I never thought I would be able to say that publicly and mean it. I am not some macho savage who needs to use women and who fears men. I have inner strength that helps me access my deep, masculine nature, allowing me to live — not just survive.

More and more, I see life as an adventure. It's an adventure that the man and the little boy in me share.

Crossing the Threshold
of Recovery:

Men in Detox

by Jeff Zeth

When my field instructor first suggested to me that I start a men's group on the hospital detoxification unit, I felt butterflies in my stomach. The men in this hospital were mostly ornery and irritable from withdrawal from cocaine and crack, or else apathetic and overmedicated with methadone, the controversial drug used to wean addicts off heroin. What could I possibly have to say to such men?

Many of them had few employment skills outside of drug dealing. Drugs had afforded them their only opportunity of bringing in an income and making a name for themselves in the world. They were uneducated, often with a prison record, and had, to say the least, a variety of motives for beginning recovery. For some, detoxifying was a "vacation"—a brief hiatus between drug binges; often they were simply homeless and were looking for an alternative to the shelter system. For others who were determined to break their addiction, detoxification was the first stage in a long recovery; for several, it was their first attempt at getting help. A few patients were also HIV-positive. Since the average length of stay is seven days and the group was held every Wednesday, most men would meet in the group only once — if at all.

The initial meetings were a forum for collective catharsis. Grief and shame around not having lived up to expected norms, as husbands and family members, was the source of many feelings of inadequacy. Several fathers in the group spoke about not being able to fill their role as providers, even as fathers who only visit their children on occasion.

Roland: I don't see my kids no more. I can't deal with it. I don't know if anyone here knows what it's like to see your kids and not even have money to buy your little girl a candy bar. (Several men nod their heads.) I'd just come down from putting about $300 worth of dope in my arm. Of course I didn't go over there to my ex-wife's place right away. Cause I never, ever will let my kids see me high in front of them — I did that once, and it was like, "Daddy, what's wrong? Daddy, are you sick?" So, like, I finally went over there when it was over and took my two little girls for a walk downtown. They're terrific — one of them's three and the other's five. And we passed a newsstand, and the little one asked if she could get a candy bar. I reached in my pocket and then realized I'd shot the money. Eriberto: (Nodding, looking down on the floor) "Yup. That's fucked up."

Roland: "Jesus Christ," I said to myself, "what the hell have I become? What the hell is this?" I fucked up my marriage, I lost custody of my two girls, and now I can't even buy one of them candy?

Eriberto: (Laughing bitterly) "It's a fucked up disease."

This interchange got some of the sons of addicts talking about how drugs had become a tradition in their family. One man spoke about how he had always looked up to his brother, who had first turned him on to heroin. Now his brother was dying of AIDS and I could see the fear in his face, as he recalled watching a man he grew up with and looked up to, slowly being consumed by a horrifying disease.

Once or twice, the family drama that had shaped these men's lives unfolded again in the room. The sons of addicts began speaking to the addict fathers as if they were their own father. This time, however, there was less avoidance of true communication, more of an opportunity to open up. There was no way of reaching for a beer, or a heroin bag, or even a cigarette. Angry words flew across the room as the men's latent desire for true communion with fathers and father-figures surfaced.

I was amazed at how simply venting emotions and "commiserating" together could be of some help; it appeared to be a powerful factor for change, at least over the short term. As facilitator, it was often my job to articulate and restate these men's remarks. This not only affirmed their outrage and shock over their own actions, but also continued to draw together men such as Roland and Eriberto, as well as those who hadn't spoken but who also had experienced what was being discussed.

Most men were not able to verbalize and share their common pain. A frequent response to the challenges presented by the group was to withdraw, not only emotionally but physically also, by getting up and leaving the room on the pretext of going to the bathroom.

Help was asked of and received from the older men in the group. One afternoon, I asked, "Some of you older guys have been on drugs 20 years or longer. How do you feel about being in here with 23-year-olds who think they know it all?" To my surprise, all heads turned toward the oldest men in the group. There was quiet in the room for a brief moment — the group wanted to hear from these men. One man who had relapsed many times spoke about feeling out of place, buying heroin on the street at age 60. Another man warned the younger men to take advantage of their age now and stop while it's easier. Another man recalled his drug experiences in Vietnam, and confessed that he had never been able to adapt to civilian life after his return home. Among Vietnam veterans, this story was common.

I went into the project thinking I could accomplish very little, and I held that view right up until the first group ended. However, the group reaction after the first session was positive. Several of the men from the core group even came up to me afterward and thanked me. It was then that I realized how much even this small, seemingly insignificant step had meant to at least a few of these men. They had accepted the invitation to take emotional risks, and had come away the better for it.

I noticed how a few of the men hunched over less and held their heads up a little higher as they filed out of the room after a session. They became more talkative, hanging around outside in the hall to continue their discussions. I still wonder, sometimes, if self-esteem was the right thing to give these men at that time; drug treatment programs are often meant to be harsh and confrontational, breaking down addictive egos that will later be put back together. But, judging from my conversations with some of the men later, they were not filled with false pride or rationalization so much as with hope and an awareness that they can recover if they want to.

The widespread problem of drug abuse, and its spread among males in particular, may be a testament to the fact that the desire for initiation, and for communion with other men, is so strong and universal that men, in the absence of anything better, act out this need in destructive ways. Luigi Zoja, in his book *Drugs, Addiction, and Initiation*, compares the drug experience to an initiation. While drug addiction and initiation spring from a collective human desire, Zoja sees the drug experience as an inverted form of initiation, emphasizing death, rather than life.

Speaking to some of the men after the end of the first group, I noticed how different some voices sounded — calmer, more hopeful or determined and, perhaps, a little more trusting. No doubt a few were insincere, but there were others who obviously hadn't completely mastered the art of concealing their emotions — they sounded afraid. But it was a healthy fear, a realistic facing of what they had so long avoided. I hope, for some of these men, that group provided a good introduction to recovery, a crossing of the threshold to a long and difficult, but ultimately rewarding road.

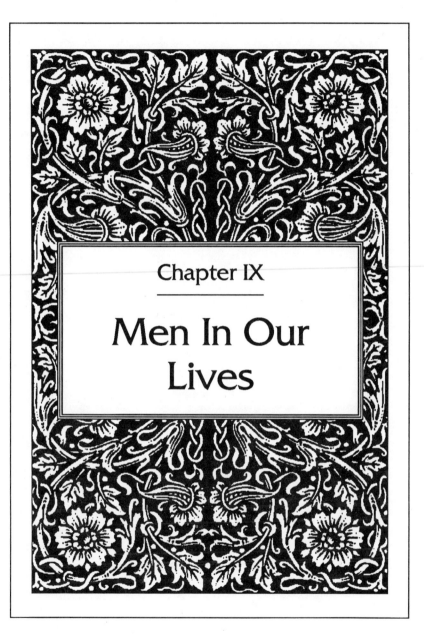

Chapter IX

Men In Our Lives

Men In Our Lives

Honored

I have been honored being my father's son ever since I was a five-year-old schoolboy. He gave me his business card to carry, Kenneth W. Donelson, Attorney-at-Law. "Keep it with you, just in case," he would say. I left home at 17. Whenever we meet now, his form of goodbye is always the same. "Do you have one of my cards?"

I always smile as I say, "Yes." After 43 years, I am still a card-carrying member of this club of two.

Richard Donelson
Austin, Texas

Homemade Ice Cream

Homemade ice cream brings back many wonderful memories of my father. He traveled quite a lot, so when he was home, all the children wanted his attention. There were 11 of us kids, so his time was quickly filled. But Daddy always made time for homemade ice cream. And I knew it was my time when he got out the ice cream maker. We didn't have an electric ice cream maker. Ours was hand-cranked, so this meant time to put in ice and salt — and plenty of time to talk. It always seemed that everyone knew this was my time, or I was the only one willing to sit there and crank the freezer all that time. In any case, the rest of the family always managed to find something else to do.

Daddy and I had many good conversations, sometimes just talking about the yard or about the clouds floating above us. Sometimes, we had more serious talks about my life. To this day, when I see an old ice cream freezer or taste the freshness of homemade ice cream, it brings back many good and comforting memories of a father I miss very much.

Kristi Heideman
Austin, Texas

The Ambassador Hotel

Shortly before the divorce, my father moved from our home into a room of the Ambassador Hotel. I came with my little suitcase to see him on weekends. The hall from the seventh-floor elevator was dark and smelled like old people. I was just eight years old. Inside the room, a Murphy bed loomed behind a set of French doors. It could nearly fill the room, and I was afraid of it. The ice box was the size of a wastebasket and usually contained half a jar of olives, some pumpernickel, old lunch meat and milk for my father's stomach.

Occasionally, Dad would miss something and go digging through the cardboard boxes that lined the perimeter of that little room. If he didn't find what he was looking for, he would curse about my mother. It stayed that way for years — the boxes, the curled-up bologna, the cursing and the black-and-white TV running endless footage of Pearl Harbor. I learned from this that women hurt men and then the men have to live in exile.

I can still see Dad standing at the sink in his boxer shorts, stirring a tumbler of water, ice and whiskey with his finger. Sometimes, he would step into the middle of the room, strike a Charles Atlas pose, slap his tightened stomach and say "pretty good for an old man, huh?" I would agree, of course. I was his only friend then, and I knew it. I learned that men are big on the outside but weak on the inside.

Sometimes, we'd play gin rummy, Dad with his drink and me with a soft drink. He'd tell me stories about when he was a boy in a military academy or about his career in politics. Then, something would move inside him, and he would have to put the newspaper up around him. I learned that men are lonely, but do not tell each other. I miss my Dad now — and I missed him then.

Stewart Warren
Taos, New Mexico

First Tears

It was one of those crisp November mornings when you decide to gas up your car without a jacket on and regret every stubborn minute your hand is wrapped around the pump handle. But Texan, you tough it out. So the drive into work is as routine as usual, except your brain is feeling full — pressing against your skull. All you can abide is the engine; no radio, no self-help tapes.

I was remembering something I'd read about a woman in group therapy who had told about her mother's kicking her in the stomach when she was a small girl. The woman had related this account of abuse with a smile on her face. The pain behind that smile must have been horrible. I thought then about a familiar subject: forgiveness. I had let go of all my childhood horrors so I could get on with the process of figuring out how best to live. Then I remembered my dad in one of his rages.

I don't remember what it was about, but what I did recall was that he had knocked me to the floor. Like slow-motion replay I remembered. He raised his leg like he was going to smash a soup can flat, and planted his foot in my testicles. I could not recall the pain — physical pain is merciful that way — but I could remember my absolute astonishment at the cruelty of the act. That and the look on his face as his raging mask of curled lips and bulging eyes did a contorted dance through shock and fear and a different kind of anger. Then he asked me if I was all right.

How I answered yes, I'll never know. It seemed to relieve him of his responsibility — nipped close the budding guilt — at least in my eyes. He left me there on the floor; I was bewildered and hurt, with another turn added to the straight path the soul should take. One more byway that would cause me years of delay, trying to find my way back.

And in the remembering, sudden, foreign tears. I was so surprised I had to pull off the road and marvel at this cleansing flow. With the cessation of tears, joy. In sight of the path again. Then, and only then, did I feel I truly released and forgave my father. Those being the first tears I can remember, I wonder how many more will be shed to wash it all away.

Michael McKeown
Austin, Texas

playing

We met in my script. I drank your blood, you waited
    for my flight through barred windows, I gave you
        small animals to suck dry.
In my script, middle of Act Two, I killed you: "Master!
    Master!"   I broke your neck.

We liked each other. Boy afternoons, at your house
    on the hill, we shouted down the noonless
        moans of drying old people.
The rest home vanished in ritual Icees, Big Hunks,
    and breath-squeezing Playboys.

And catch. Baseball or Frisbee, something to release,
    to watch fly, to receive, to grasp, something
        to connect us through increasing
distances. Blue Frisbees, balls and gloves, flying saucers:
    we threw days in mid-air.

Like the plays, the characters, four-a-year at least.
    Our voices tossed words, flung them through the sky!
        We ran madly after cues!
Miller, Shakespeare, Stoppard, Albee and Kopit—
    my mouth to yours and back!

Fastasyoucan shotgun mind-races, or laughing,
    dropping, "I always get those two mixed up!"
        And in the joy of the line,
the spoken heart of the monologue, a Frisbee spun,
    your hand to mine and back.

Competition was there, too. Whose part was bigger,
    flew straighter, had the best scenes, ran faster,
        got the laughs, made the play, got
the girl? "What a birthday present! Nice Toss!" "You mean you
    kissed. . .
    her?" "Behind the back! Oops!"

In London, airmail lines from your girlfriend arrived,
    saying she was my girlfriend. You took it
        well. We got together, tossed
a few jokes about stage combat, and then played Frisbee
    on your hill, like old times.

Anyone could see the disk try to spin backwards,
    or measure the wingless arc of young men's
        uneven aging, noting
relationships between slope and length, trust and deceit.
    Act Two.   I broke your youth.

Six years deeper, yet still wingless, the rock threw you
    into Yosemite's snowswollen blood.
        Like a tumor, your backpack
mysteriously enlarged, bloated with this drowning.
    Had I seen you fall, what

could I have done? Thrown your name?
            Mark! Mark! Catch! The light
    circle would have floated dry above you,
        floated wet beside you, kept

                you
cold company, left me behind.   Your family
    asked me to speak at your
        memorial, at the theater. I stayed away,
    so afraid of our heavy, dripping death.

        The angry sky had fallen,
            out of the tossing blue...

D.A. Elliott
Sacramento, California

My Brother

My brother collected matchbooks.
Here I am in his apartment.
By now I'm forty-one and I like
the word middle-aged. It's dark
and foreboding, but has a tradition
of troubadours.

His collection has grown small
in a basket, one match struck
from the pink book from the Ocean Club.
I recall my brother with his drawer full
of the world, Las Vegas, Palm Springs,
Miami. And his solid steady path into that life,
college afternoons working at the store
to learn the clothing business.
He married right. He pursued.
My brother wore the mensch suit
better than anybody.

His collection has grown small
in a basket, one match struck
from the pink book from the Ocean Club.
I recall my brother with his drawer full
of the world, Las Vegas, Palm Springs,
Miami. And his solid steady path into that life,
college afternoons working at the store
to learn the clothing business.
He married right. He pursued.
My brother wore the mensch suit
better than anybody.

Joan Logghe
Espanola, New Mexico

Older Brothers and Newer Brothers

My earliest lessons in masculinity were gleaned from observing my three brothers, who range in age from 10 to 13 years older than me. When I was a child, I marveled at them during their glory days of adolescence and young adulthood. I saw them as BIGGER and MORE POWERFUL than me. There was considerable evidence of this in my eyes — their muscles, their sports trophies, their pocket money, their girlfriends. I mimicked their style in an effort to bridge the gap of years so that I could be recognized and respected as an equal, rather than as a skinny kid brother. I cuffed my jeans. I greased my hair. I smoked cigarettes. I did not understand that I was locking myself into an impossible task — being a decade older than I was.

Over the years, I have been fortunate to find many newer brothers. We are not brothers by birth, we are brothers of the spirit. Some are older and some are younger. I am their equal by accepting who I am — not by trying to be someone I am not. We share. We laugh. We cry. We sing. We dream. The lesson in masculinity that I glean from my newer brothers is that we are all still growing.

Bob Carty,
Evanston, Illinois

To My Grandfather, Hub Melchior

As I recall my grandfather, I have this mental picture of a heavyset man, wearing a tattersall plaid shirt, and a tan, wraparound shop apron, the kind that tied in the back. His favorite drink was his John Paul Jones, and he always smoked Pall Malls. Growing up with him right next door to me and my parents in Los Angeles in the early 1950s was quite an experience. When I would go with him on various short business trips around Los Angeles, he would always introduce me as, "Thisw is my grandson, of whom I am well pleased." For years, I had no idea where he had come up with that phrase. All I knew was that it made me feel special every time I heard it.

On one of our trips to an old hardware store, while Grandpa did his business with the store owner, I was enthralled looking at some red maple baseball bats with white grip tape. I never said a word, but as we were about to leave the store, the owner came up and gave me one of the bats, a gift not only to me but to my grandfather as well. Grandpa was the type of man who did a lot for others just because he enjoyed giving and rarely ever requested anything in return. I suspect that this bat was a way of showing honor and thanks to my grandfather.

My grandfather became ill after a stroke, and was moved to his old family home in Mt. Angel, Oregon, where he died. I was asked to be an altar boy in his funeral mass and burial. I had been attending a parochial elementary school in Los Angeles at the time; I was in the third grade. In those days, the priests and sisters were really good at being able to shame me. This shame was to a point that I was so afraid of messing up something during the funeral mass that I declined the offer and merely watched the service. For years after this I would regret that choice. I sorely wished that I could have permitted myself to take part in that ceremony and in that way say goodbye to my grandfather. I recall my grandfather's brother, who was a priest and who officiated at the service, closing the ceremonies at the cemetery by saying that my grandfather had been "the best brother a brother could be."

Years would pass. I and my own family would move from Los Angeles to Oregon. When my grandmother died, my youngest son was asked to be a part of her funeral, which was held in the same church as my grandfather's. At first, my son did not want to participate in the service, he too fearing that he might do something wrong. I recalled my story to him and he decided to participate. Both he and I were pleased that he did, and now often share stories of my grandfather.

Today as a social worker I sit in my office hearing other men talk about their own grandfathers, remembering and holding onto that contact that I still have with my grandfather. A picture of him and me sits on a table in my office. My grandfather was not just a grandfather, but rather one of my first true teachers and my first true mentor, who will long be remembered and cherished.

Jim Alderson
Salem, Oregon

My Uncle

We were a good match, my Uncle Larry and I. I didn't have a father. He didn't have a son. I don't think I was ever conscious of it at the time, but looking back I know he filled that role for me. And I'd like to think that I did for him. I can't say for sure because he died nine years ago. He was only 48, and neither of us was prepared for him to be gone. But still, for 25 years, my uncle was one of the only men I liked and trusted.

I have many memories of times we spent together, too many to share here. Playing, laughing, joking — many good times. Sports, in particular, were a big part of my relationship with Larry. Each year as the seasons passed, my Uncle and I would talk over the rise — actually it was more often the demise — of Chicago's sports teams. We talked baseball, basketball, and most importantly, football. We were both Bears fans, through and through. In Chicago, season tickets to Bears games were a valued commodity. People bequeathed their seats in their wills. My uncle had season tickets, which always gave him a special kind of aura to me (along with the basketball trophy). As a kid, it was my uncle who took me to Bears games.

The Bears of my youth were almost always pretty bad, but Larry and I loved them anyway. Larry always had his favorite players — Dick Butkus and Mike Ditka are the two he talked about all the time. He'd tell me stories about them and their teammates, as if he knew them as friends. To this day, I don't know if he really did or not. But I was impressed.

Suddenly, in 1980 (or thereabouts), my uncle announced that he was "giving up his Bears tickets." I guess he was tired of the seemingly endless losing seasons. I was shocked. It seemed almost a betrayal of our trust. But by then I'd already left Chicago and was living in Ann Arbor, and I never voiced my feelings about the tickets.

When my uncle died of a heart attack in 1982, the Bears still weren't very good. It seemed too ironic and unfair that only three years later they were in the Super Bowl, heroes to the whole country. All those years my uncle and I had stood behind them as they fumbled and bumbled their way through the seasons. And then, three years after he dies, they're world champs. I thought of Larry during the Super Bowl. Even then, it brought tears to my eyes (in truth it still does, five years later). I don't know who Walter Payton was playing the game for (his mother?), but for me, that game was for Larry.

He wasn't perfect, my uncle. As I've gone through my own rediscovery in the last few years, I've learned more about Larry and the rest of my family. Many of the behaviors I have struggled with myself, I can see were his as well. Looking back, it seems that Larry — like me — spent much of his life going back and forth, trying to please those around him, then rebelling and trying to stake out what he wanted for himself. I think he had a hard time standing up for what he wanted, especially with the women in his life (I can relate). And I think he spent a lot of energy trying to make the women around him happy — his mother, his wife, his sister (my mother), his daughters.

Unlike me, my uncle always had many male friends in his life. In fact, he had a whole set of them — "the O'Keefe Gang," they called themselves — who stayed friends from grammar school on. Because I never trusted men, other than Larry, I could never really understand this friendship. But the O'Keefe Gang really did stick together. I saw them all at Larry's funeral. They're still together today.

Despite our closeness, Larry and I really had only one "man-to-man" talk. It was a few years before he died, and I was visiting Chicago from Ann Arbor. I'd finished school and was working in a restaurant. Life seemed good to me then. But Larry was having a tough time of it. His marriage was on the rocks, and his self esteem was as low as I'd ever seen it. We went out for a beer together, and for the first time we talked as peers — commiserating, supporting, and sharing, something other than the Bears. It was the start of a new era in our relationship. Sadly, we never got the chance to take it any further.

My Uncle died suddenly of a heart attack at the young age of 48, in the middle of a game of racquetball. I (and I think the rest of my family as well) was in shock. He'd seemed so full of life.

I'll never forget the day he died. I had just opened my own store in Ann Arbor a week earlier, working 18-hour days to get the place off the ground. It was near the end of one of those marathon days when the phone rang. "It's for you," whoever answered the phone said. "It's your sister." I took the phone, totally unprepared for what I was about to hear.

"Uncle Larry had a heart attack," she said quietly. She paused for a second, and I remember waiting for her to go on. "And he died."

I cried at Larry's funeral, probably the first time I'd done so in ages. In fact, I'm crying now as I write this.

I miss Larry more than I can say.

Ari Weinzweig
Ann Arbor, Michigan

New Boots, Big Steps

Biopsy positive: "Just a few cancer cells in the middle of the polyp. Look, you're 83. Go and take a trip with your wife, travel for a couple of years, what the hell."

He gave us our first taste of exhilarating freedom and power, the best vacation a kid ever had. Uncle knew everyone at Coney Island, and once during the '50s when we were on a trip to New York from the Deep South, he took our family to Coney.

There was no Disney-anything in those days. Coney Island had the biggest and best amusement park in the world. He announced that as a treat, he was going to let my brother and me have three turns on any and every ride we wanted. Three turns!

I can still hear the calliope's old-fashioned (even then) tootle, smell the caramel apples and sweet cotton candy and the gasoline-powered rides and the fresh, clean breath of the ocean. I can hear the barkers and the motors and see the lights and the twisting, clanging rides. People everywhere, kids, fun, good smells, good-humored New York chaos.

We started with little rides. Easy rides. The Tilt-A-Whirl, the Ferris wheel. We were veterans of small-town carnivals and county fairs, and we had long since outgrown their thrills — except for unadvertised thrills, such as we had once in Georgia when we glanced down at the rickety bolt holding the swinging Ferris-wheel chair onto the framework, realizing that the two halves of the frame were not put together tightly enough when the carnival was set up, and the chair was hanging by the last 1/8-inch of the bolt. That made us nervous about Ferris wheels forever. But we trusted the competent New Yorkers at Coney. Coney Island's rides did not have to be moved, anyway, and they were inspected by New York City building inspectors, one of whom was Uncle Lundy. We had faith.

We delighted in the parachute ride out on the beach. Mama could not look up at us, but we were ecstatic as the parachutes floated down and we saw all of Coney Island, including the roller coaster on the far edge, and saw much of Brooklyn, the skyscrapers of Manhattan and the Atlantic Ocean.

We grew more and more daring. Three rides? Did he really mean three rides on each? He did, but no more than three rides. We felt important and powerful and we did not mind waiting in line each time. We could do anything we dared to do. Uncle smiled the little, mysterious smile he alone had. He enjoyed watching us experience our new freedom, our excitement, our breathless courage as we worked up to the Biggest Roller Coaster in the World, the Cyclone.

It was a tall, gorgeous and hilly thing, made of crisscrossed timbers that were painted white. The cars roared by faster than wind, seeming to pull a sound-banner of wheel clatter and rider screams. The Cyclone was huge and scary and tempting. The old carnival Ferris wheel had made us little cynics, but we clung to the assurance that no one had ever been hurt on the Cyclone. Uncle was the building inspector, and was meticulous in everything he did. We trusted him.

We finally reached the front of the line. We were the youngest riders, but we measured up on the measuring stick. My mother exclaimed to no avail to my father, aunt and uncle. We were clamped into our car by a U-shaped bar pushed down onto our laps by an energetic, young, Italian man. We tested it; we were safely locked in.

"Doncha try ta stand up, OK?"

Not a chance! We were excited and scared enough as it was.

At last all were clamped in, someone yelled a signal, and the car began to chug up the highest hill — slowly, slowly. We were higher than the parachutes! We gradually crested the hill, barely moving at all, then everyone moaned as we flew face downward into the abyss.

Down down down unbearably fast can't stop fast, everyone screaming, then at the last second before doom — a lurch, a climb, a hesitation, another free fall! Wind, roar, clatter, scream, delight of survival, delicious terror, the feeling of physical peril made safe mentally, joyful rocking side-to-side, up, down, around, the crisscrossed timbers all around us now and blurring past. Then the cars roll into port and we are released, wobbly-legged and breathless, to run and wait in line again. My mother aghast, her relief short-lived; "You want to that again?"

We rode the Cyclone three times that day. We could have ridden it forever. When our last ride was over and we were all heading home, I remember my mother's undisguised relief, my father's disguised relief, and Uncle's characteristic little smile. We felt like great adventurers triumphantly returning home. We had, after all, conquered considerable terror.

"Thank you, thank you, thank you, Uncle Lundy!"

"You liked that, hunh? I'm glad you liked that."

Mama gave Uncle a sidelong look of mingled exasperation and pride. Her older brother had helped her fledglings spread their wings and fly a little, long before she thought they were ready. That is what a good uncle can do — an uncle who loves your children almost as much as you do, but who can see them as people, not babies, can take them whitewater rafting or give them a glorious day at Coney Island.

Years later, when I had become a mother myself, I stood in line in Houston's hot, muggy summer to ride a replica of the Cyclone they had built at AstroWorld. I waited two hours for a two-minute ride that was worth the wait and the reminder that you are never too old or too young to challenge yourself.

Now Uncle is facing perhaps the greatest challenge of his life. All of us in the family, all of the children, grandchildren, nieces and nephews whose characters he helped build with his example and his encouragement are standing by him now. And he is still teaching.

Yvonne Baron Estes
Austin, Texas

A New Plea to Men

Flying Boys,
Flying Boys,
Fly away home.

Alight on my doorstep.

Await on the ground.

Wild Men,
Come around.

Dear sweet
Smell of men
Filter through.

Leave your mothers behind.

Face the Darkness.
Face the Darkness.

Face the Darkness
With us.

Peggy O'Mara
Santa Fe, New Mexico

Contributors

James M. Alderson. A licensed clinical social worker from Salem, Oregon, Mr. Alderson's practice, while still fairly general in nature, has increasingly focused on men's issues in recent years. His interests include traveling with family and friends and motorcycle restoration.

Marvin Allen. A psychotherapist with a special interest in men's issues, Mr. Allen sponsors numerous men's groups including wilderness gatherings in Texas and other locations in the U.S. He is founder and director of the Texas Men's Institute in San Antonio and a frequent spokesman on men's issues through the national media. He is the author of *In the Company of Men*, to be published in late 1992.

Rich Armington. A psychotherapist in private practice in Austin, Texas, Mr. Armington is interested in how systems affect individual development and how we can heal the wounds that keep us separate from the ones we love. He recently finished a children's book on the subject of a boy becoming a man, to be published in late 1992.

Carolyn Baker. A psychotherapist and counselor in Santa Rosa, California, Ms Baker is particularly interested in Jungian depth psychology and bridging the gap between male and female through dialogue. She is working on a book, *Wounded and Well: Cherishing the Process of Transformation*, which includes a chapter on healing the wounded feminine and masculine.

Shepherd Bliss. A psychologist, Mr. Bliss teaches at JFK University in the San Francisco Bay area and directs the Kokopelli Traveling Lodge, a group of ceremonial artists who tour the U.S., Canada, and Europe. Mr. Bliss also helps direct the Sons of Orpheus. A contributor to over a dozen books, he was the first to apply the term "mythopoetic" to the men's movement. A free sample of his *Men, Gender and Soul Newsletter* is available from P.O. Box 1133, Berkeley, CA 94701, (610) 549-1938.

Robert Bly. A nationally recognized poet, author, and lecturer, Mr. Bly's best-selling book, *Iron John: A Book About Men*, has presented a mythopoetic vision of men and their current place in modern culture to hundreds of thousands of readers. Other books include *What Have I Ever*

197

Lost by Dying?: Collected Prose Poems; *Remembering James Wright*; and *American Poetry: Wildness and Domesticity.*

Bill Bruzy. Currently the director of the Austin Men's Center, Mr. Bruzy has a Master's degree in health sciences from Johns Hopkins University School of Public Health. He is a certified therapist with specialization in eating disorders and an avid drummer.

Bob Carty. In addition to a private counseling practice in Evanston, Illinois, Mr. Carty works as a trainer in the Clinical Training Program for Addictions Counselors and is a member of ACOA. Mr. Carty's two children "... are wonderful guides for me to discover the areas that I need to work upon." He has been a member of a leaderless men's group for the past year and is particularly interested in men's issues as they apply to addictions counseling.

Gordon Clay. Editor of *Men's Resource Hotline Calendar* and founder of the National Men's Resource Center in the San Francisco Bay Area, Mr. Clay has been involved in men's work since the 1970s when he established The Father's Network for discussing the problems and joys of parenting. He has planned, organized, published and talked about men's issues in many settings since that time. He currently sponsors retreats for men and women with special emphasis on relationships, dealing with anger and rites of initiation.

Barry Cooney. A leader of the National Men's Workshop, Mr. Cooney is author and editor of *Man Alive!*, New Mexico's journal of men's wellness. (P.O. Box 40300, Albuquerque NM 87196).

Jed Diamond. Author, psychotherapist, and addictions specialist in Willits, California, Mr. Diamond has written *The Warriors Journey Home: Healing Men's Addictions, Healing the Planet*; *Looking for Love in all the Wrong Places: Overcoming Romantic and Sexual Addictions*; and *Inside Out: Becoming My Own Man.* He conducts workshops and training throughout the country, often with his wife, Carlin.

Richard Donelson. Dr. Donelson is an MD living in Austin, Texas, with specialties in public health, epidemiological investigation and administrative medicine.

Dave Elliott. With interests in poetry, music, politics, drumming, storytelling, and his son Stephen, Mr. Elliott lists James Hillman as a favorite author. He lives in Sacramento, California and has published poetry in *Poet News* and *Sunseeds*.

Yvonne Baron Estes. Ms Estes is a college instructor at Austin Community College in Austin, Texas and a writer of poetry, short stories, essays, and articles. She enjoys gardening and nature.

Robert German. A poet and teacher of writing at Austin Community College, Austin Texas, Mr. German's poetry has appeared in *Gusher, The Green World, Harvest, Arx, The Weather Report, The Southwest Review* and *The Kansas Quarterly*.

David Gilmore. Mr. Gilmore, a professor of anthropology at SUNY at Stony Brook and Hunter College, lists interests in cultural anthropology, rites-of-passage and men's issues. He has authored *Aggression and Community, Manhood in the Making*, and *People of the Plain*.

Lyman Grant. Publisher and managing editor of *MAN! Magazine* since 1990, Mr. Grant is a poet and teacher of writing at Austin Community College. His writing has appeared in the *Texas Observer, the Dallas Morning News* and *Texas Books and Reviews, Icarus Review*. He served as the book review editor of the *Texas Humanist* and edited *New Growth*, a book of Texas short stories for Corona Press. He co-edited *The Letters of Roy Bedichek* with Dr. Bill Owens for University of Texas Press.

James Hagen. A priest in the Episcopal Church in New York City, Mr. Hagen enjoys running, playing piano, and playing racquetball in his leisure hours. He holds a Master's degree in Sacred Theology from Episcopal Divinity School.

Jonathan Holden. Serving as the poet-in-residence at Kansas State University, Mr. Holden's book of poetry, *Against Paradise*, is published by University of Utah Press.

Bill Jeffers. Bill has been writing poetry, playing percussion, performing, and earning a living doing a variety of strange and interesting things in Austin, Texas for more than 20 years. He is currently working on the publication of a children's Christmas book, *How Rancho Rugtabaga Helped Holy Mackerel Celebrate Christmas*. His poem, *The Great Hunt*, is available on audio tape by sending $6 to him at 1507 Kinney #205, Austin, TX 78704

David Kramer. A lawyer by profession, Mr. Kramer serves as assistant editor of *MAN! Magazine* in his spare time. A keen interest in Jungian psychology has led Mr. Kramer to his examinations of dreams and fables of our modern life. He lives in Austin, Texas with his seven-year-old daughter, Willa.

John Lee. Author of *The Flying Boy: Healing the Wounded Man* and *I Don't Want to Be Alone*, Mr. Lee is a nationally recognized spokesman in the men's movement and the fields of codependency and addictive relationships. He is the founder of the Austin Men's Center and a presenter of lectures and workshops for clinics and treatment centers throughout the U.S.

Joan Logghe. A poet and writer from Espanola, New Mexico, Ms Logghe has published her poems in numerous literary and general interest magazines including *Writer's Digest*, *The Taos Review* and *Sing Heavenly Muse!* She conducts writing workshops and is poetry editor for *Mothering* magazine. She received the National Endowment for the Arts Poetry Fellowship in 1991.

Thom McFarland. A teacher of English at Austin Community College, backpacker, swimmer and self-styled rabble-rouser, Mr. McFarland has published his writing in *Mothering*, *Journeyman*, *Men Talk*, *The Austin Chronicle* and the *Austin American-Statesman*. He lives in Austin, Texas and is currently working on a book about disposable daddies.

Jim McGrath. A poet and visual artist living in Santa Fe, New Mexico, Mr. McGrath's narrative poetry was presented in the PBS Indian Artists Series: "Loloma," "Scholder," "Houser," "Hardin," "Gorman," and "Lonewolf and Morning Flower." He has written a book of poetry, *A Crack in the Wall*, and been published in various books and magazines, including *Arizona Highways*, *Crosswinds* and *Language and Art in the Navaho Universe*.

Michael McKeown. With interests in music, art and athletics, Mr. McKeown lives in Austin, Texas where he works as a training consultant.

200

In his educational history, Mr. McKeown is careful to include his service in the Marine Corps (". . .that's an education!")

Peggy O'Mara. Editor and publisher of *Mothering* magazine in Santa Fe, New Mexico, Ms O'Mara lists poetry, children, flowers, and a better world as her prime interests. She has published a book of essays entitled *The Way Back Home.*

Ron Phillips. A writer living in Fort Worth, Texas, Mr. Phillips began writing professionally at age 45 as a result of insights gained through his recovery. He is currently working on a book, *From Shame to Manhood* (concerning men's recovery from childhood abuse) and a screenplay entitled *The Mockingbird and the Crow.*

Randolph Severson. A writer and therapist in Dallas, Texas, Mr. Severson is particularly interested in issues of adoption, fostering, mentoring and patterns of child raising. He has published books on children's issues and adoption including *Adoption as a Spiritual Path; The Inaccessible Pinnacle: Further Essays on Adoption*; and *Adoption: Charms and Rituals for Healing.*

James Sniechowski. Founder and director of The Menswork Center in Los Angeles, California, Mr. Sniechowski combines his writing, speaking and leadership activities for men's issues with workshops and lectures conducted with his wife, Judith Sherven. Their work concerns the interactions of men and women, the impact of the men's movement on women, and the problems caused by the dominance-submission relationship model. Mr. Sniechowski's writing has been published in a variety of magazines, journals, and newspapers including *Journeyman, Los Angeles Daily News, Barrister* and *Sober Times.*

Stewart S. Warren. A therapist in private practice in Taos, New Mexico, Mr. Warren's interests lie with Native American spirituality, the development of human consciousness and the beauty of the land. He notes, "We cannot be shamed into right-relationship without self, our community, or our earth. Through self-love, we discover that our hearts know the way home."

Ari Weinzweig. Owner of Zingerman's Delicatessen and a loyal Bears fan, Mr. Weinzweig finds time to write, read Russian history, run, and study foods of the world for his popular Ann Arbor, Michigan restaurant.

201

Ric Williams. Dubbing himself a corporate gadfly in his office job, Mr. Williams' interests lie in poetry and more poetry. He is: Son of Bill and Gloria; Husband of Christy Kale; Father to Kady Rain; Uncle for April, Hannah and Rebecca; Brother to Becky Denise; Man for the Future; King of his Dreams; A Friend to You; Hero, Villain, Fool, Sage — and lives in Austin, Texas.

Jeffrey Zeth. Working as an alcoholism therapist in Brooklyn, New York, Mr. Zeth published "Men and the Mythopoetic Tradition" in *The Quest*. He enjoys Italian food, flirting, Stan Rogers' songs, Rick Moranis' movies, the Catholic liturgy, and freedom.